UPSKILL, RESKILL, THRIVE

OPTIMIZING LEARNING AND DEVELOPMENT IN THE WORKPLACE

by

James McKenna, EdD

ISBN (paperback) 978-1-930583-96-2

ISBN (ebook) 978-1-930583-97-9

Library of Congress Control Number: 2022944716

Cover design by Martha Kennedy

Book design and production by Westchester Education Services

Published by CAST Professional Publishing, an imprint of CAST, Inc., Wakefield, Massachusetts, USA

For information about special discounts for bulk purchases, please email publishing@cast.org or visit publishing.cast.org.

Dedication

For my wife, who has always seen more in me than I have in myself and who gave me the space and grace to write, learn, and grow. This is all your fault.

For my children, who loved me enough to let me write in peace, without complaint. You can do anything if you are willing to work hard, listen to sound advice, and admit when you have more work to do. McKennas never give up!

For the McKennas and the Fosters, who wonder what it is I actually do and patiently listen as I prattle on about science, design, and behavior change. I hope this helps fill in the gaps!

Contents

MAKING THE UDL JOURNEY

It's my honor to introduce to you James McKenna's insightful and practical book that explores the application of Universal Design for Learning (UDL) to the learning and development (L&D) field. While UDL has its roots in the K–12 environment, James recognizes the value of UDL to help guide L&D practices to better meet the diverse needs of today's workforce. You hold in your hands the means to intentionally create equitable, accessible learning environments filled with expert learners. Imagine an empowered workforce that is purposefully driven to learn, share, and improve.

Based on research into the brain and learning, UDL is both a framework that addresses the **why**, **what**, and **how** of learning and a heuristic process to help you enhance and accelerate learning in your workplace. UDL recognizes the variability of learners and the physical, emotional, and cognitive barriers that exist in today's corporate environment and provides clear guidelines on how to overcome them. UDL recognizes the potential of people by actively removing barriers, making the hidden aspects of learning explicit, and empowering learners to better understand themselves while taking ownership of their learning. Its implementation involves a mindset shift—a culture change—that challenges your assumptions and beliefs about learners and learning. As such, UDL isn't a lockstep program. It isn't a to-do list. Just as each learner is unique, so too is your UDL journey.

My UDL journey began in 2004, as a K–12 educator and later as a professional development (PD) provider across North America and the president of the Inclusive Learning Network of the International Society for Technology in Education (ISTE). It was clear that UDL could positively affect instructional design, course design, and adult professional learning, moving far beyond its K–12 roots. This led me to incorporate Universal Design for Learning when I was senior manager of learning design and delivery at Walmart. There, my team designed learning for 90,000 associates across Canada. Together, we focused on employees' existing skills and abilities and targeted simpler (and faster) ways for them to learn. We also recognized the aspects of UDL we were already including, such as hands-on activities, interactive problem solving, and providing options and choice in how we take in information or perform tasks.. Over time, we acknowledged that many of the problems we saw (such as lack of engagement, lack of retention, and so on) were internal to the design, not external to the learner.

I've been on my UDL journey, committed to celebrating diversity, building equity, and empowering learners, for almost 20 years. The UDL Guidelines—a detailed, research-based resource for implementing the framework—are both the foundation and the heart of that journey. And I'm still learning. Reading James' book, I had many "a-ha!" moments when my prior understanding shifted, connections were made, and my understanding grew. Here is a snapshot of ideas that resonated with me. You will no doubt find many more of your own.

Barriers: James asks you to consider the barriers in your current learning environment through the creation of "journey maps", which consider in depth the learner's perspective when designing a learning experience. At Walmart, we collaboratively developed routines and subsequent training through the inclusion of personas and a "day in the life" activities. Journey maps go deeper by bringing a variety of points of view together (including, when possible, that of the actual learner) to review the existing learning assets, experiences, technologies, and spaces to find and address the barriers and opportunities that exist.

Learner Expertise: James explains the importance of creating a company culture based on developing learner expertise, during which learners actively seek out new learning rather than passively complete the bare minimum to meet training requirements. As you work toward the goal of learner expertise, make it a priority to share what you are doing and why. Help all leaders understand UDL. Help them make the connection to their learning and development. Although change won't happen overnight, the importance of continuously sharing the concept of UDL is as important as designing with UDL. This focus is vital if UDL is to become part of your learning culture.

UDL Layers: The richness of UDL is often overlooked because of its "checklist" appearance (columns and rows). Often, when one is new to UDL, one focuses solely on the vertical, the actions that are "instructor" led and owned. James expertly leads you through the vertical guidelines and checkpoints and then moves to the horizontal layers (access, build, internalize), making each aspect of UDL understandable. In the Appendix (the most useful appendix ever!), James then provides you with practical suggestions of what UDL might look like for each checkpoint by asking questions through the L&D lens. Essentially, James provides you with the why, what, and how to help you start your UDL journey.

Safety: UDL explicitly asks educators to "foster a safe place to learn and take risks" (Checkpoint 7.3). James does a brilliant job of describing how to create psychological safety and then provide active and ongoing support for people as they take risks from speaking publicly, to challenging assumptions, to pursuing a new career. To use a swimming analogy, many learning organizations equate safety with staying in the shallow end of the pool, rather than providing swimmers with a variety of paths for learning to swim, various supports (including each other) to keep afloat, and consistent modeling, reflection, and reinforcement so everyone can learn to swim in the deep end safely and with confidence.

Next Steps: No matter where you are in your UDL journey, from novice to expert, this book will support you as you shift the focus from problems to people. James' unique framing (and explanation) of UDL within the L&D context and his use of personal stories and thoughtful questions and examples will not overwhelm you (or make you feel guilty), but will encourage you to make changes to your corporate learning structure, one countermeasure at a time.

In whatever way you came to this book (and UDL), and indeed, however you access it, use it, and engage with it, you hold both a framework and a heuristic guide that will help you create within your organization a robust learning community that recognizes, celebrates, and leverages the diversity of today's workforce.

—Kendra Grant

A NEW APPROACH TO LEARNING AND DEVELOPMENT

Welcome to the journey into a new way for learning and development professionals to support learning. We're at a crucial stage here because I have only a short time to convince you that you're in the right place. You have a problem, and your search for solutions has brought you here, but now, I need to assure you that you're on the right path and that this is the next step in your journey.

My guess is that you're here to learn how better to foster learning in individuals, teams, and organizations. Maybe you're new to learning and development (L&D for short), or maybe you're a seasoned pro who has banked years of encouraging and supporting all sorts of workers across many different sectors, industries, and types of organizations. Maybe you're somewhere in between. In any case, in this time of seismic social and economic change, you're more than likely looking to take your practice to a new, more impactful level and want to make learning more meaningful, informative, and actionable. You may also want to make sure that all your learners can grow in their work and take pride and ownership in their own improvement and that their supervisors will see the value in the support you've provided.

But I have no doubt that, like all of us in the L&D field, you've been running into some obstacles. This is to be expected. Deep, meaningful learning can be hard, and supporting it is equally so. Just as all gardeners know they can't make a flower grow, only create the conditions that promote growth, we know that we can't *make* people learn. However, if we understand how people learn, why they learn, and the variability that exists within those spaces, we can begin to create the conditions in which learning thrives. In this way, we acknowledge that learning is done *by* people, not *to* them.

Fostering learning may seem daunting, but we have one huge advantage: People want to learn. In fact, they're wired for it, and when they fail to learn, it's because something is getting in the way. There's a barrier, maybe more than one. Our job is to identify those barriers—whatever's getting in the way of learning—and either remove them or help the learners address them. I like to think of this challenge to remove obstacles as providing countermeasures—options and supports that address barriers to learning—and teach the learners to use such tools and techniques in order to take ownership of their learning. That's right, the most effective L&D professional is one who not only helps folks learn content but also teaches them *how* to learn: strategically, efficiently, and effectively.

When people know how to learn, they own their improvements and we become their partners. Learning becomes what they do rather than something done to them. In our roles as L&D professionals, we support and guide these efforts. The impact of such partnership cannot be overstated; it has the power to allow people to become their best selves in their work, thereby lifting individual, team, and organizational performance to new heights.

This idea of partnership runs contrary to traditional performance improvement; indeed, the inertia of tradition and "how it's always been done" can be hard to overcome. The thing is, the pandemic overcame it for us. Though the ills of COVID-19 are numerous and, in many cases, tragic, a line of demarcation has been drawn. Just as historical events—World War II, the advent of the internet, and 9/11—forever changed our social and economic landscapes, the COVID-19 pandemic will forever be coupled with a shift in how we all conduct business. One day, we will describe many of our practices and systems as "How we did things before COVID" and "What we decided to do after COVID." For me, this reality presents us with a *huge* opportunity: We can finally unshackle ourselves from a top-down, one-size-fits-all model of professional learning and chart a new path, one that is collaborative rather than directive. We can move on from supporting learning from the inside out—designing supports in contexts that are often removed from where the learning is most needed—and focus on learning from the edges, where the work happens.

Since I began writing this book, the world, including the world of work, has changed immensely, forcing individuals and organizations to adapt in order to survive. We in L&D can't support that change alone. The pace and scope of learning that's necessary for organizations to survive, let alone thrive, is too great to be driven from the inside out. Learning can't be an abstract endeavor; people increasingly need support for learning in the flow of work. We need to partner with those closest to the work to bring forward the problems, identify and seek out the necessary knowledge and skills to address the workplace challenges, and guide the development of novel solutions. In short, we need to empower workers and inspire them to become *expert* learners.

You might be wondering about the term "expert learners." I've embraced the definition put forth by Harvard-affiliated neuropsychologist David Rose, who cofounded the innovative education research organization CAST. Rose and his cofounder, Anne Meyer, define expert learners as those who know why they must learn, what they should learn next, and how they learn most effectively.[1] Expert learners assess their own capabilities (both strengths and weaknesses) and make plans to improve. They know where to find sources of needed information and guidance, as well as supports to make sense of new information. They can connect new knowledge to their own context and the greater goals of their teams and organization. They share information effectively, and they strategically apply their learning to make measurable improvements in their performance.

How does helping develop expert learners benefit you, the L&D professional? By developing expert learners, we are better business partners, able to support learning where it's happening most often and likely at the most impactful times. Expert learners are more engaged, with a clear sense of purpose, and they are able to sustain high levels of effort and persistence when work and learning get hard. Expert learners are more efficient because they know where to find what they need in order to do what they have to do. Finally, expert learners are effective because they can think and act strategically and adjust as needed to get hard things done and done well.[2] How's that for a return on investment?

Further, by understanding the role of the environment in fostering and sustaining learning, we can design better learning experiences. We can leverage the insights and experiences of our learners to make our designs more relevant, inclusive, and impactful. Finally, we can transition from an "us-them" paradigm to a united "we," a partnership in performance improvement and organizational success.

I promise, although I am offering you a new approach to your work, it's not an approach that requires a lot more work on your part. Indeed, it requires more of a shift in how you think about your role and approaching how you can help your people own their own learning. I'll share strategies and resources to support this shift and show you how to cultivate the necessary buy-in to galvanize individuals, teams, departments, and organizations. Just like on a path, we'll take it one step at a time, and at times, we'll pause to look back at how far we've come and the opportunities still waiting ahead.

This journey can help you to reinvent what learning looks like—for yourself and for your people. To begin, we're going to examine what the full sequence of learning looks like in the modern world of work: know your learners, know your environment, make an emotional connection, make an intellectual connection, make a strategic connection, and put your learning to work (see Figure In.1). We'll look at how the pace of change as well as the need for increased personalization are making plain the inadequacy of the traditional, top-down, inside-out model of learning. We'll look at the characteristics of the modern adult learner and see how, in the process of becoming expert learners, you can leverage the collective power of your people and empower them to innovate and thrive.

From there, I'm going to show you how empowering your people to become expert learners not only motivates them to adapt, upskill, reskill, and actually enjoy learning, but also provides the organization a way to become more productive, agile, and therefore more successful. You will discover what makes every learner unique and how these differences reflect essential variability among learners and the vast array of influences that make learning such an individual phenomenon. Some of those differences among learners stem from internal forces, such as individual cognitive and emotional strengths and weaknesses; others are rooted in the environment, that is, the emotional, intellectual, and physical contexts in which the learning is happening. Indeed, these factors are what make learning— and teaching—so challenging. However, these differences are not an obstacle or problem to be solved; rather, they are assets to be leveraged.

Next, we will take what we know about an organization's needs and goals and align them with what individuals need to work better or more efficiently in their jobs. Indeed, when we are able both to discern an organization's goals and understand more clearly how to help individual people reach those goals, individuals, teams, and organizations will be able to operate at peak capacity.

To inform and support this work of understanding, engaging, and empowering our learners, we will incorporate the principles of Universal Design for Learning (UDL), a research-based framework specifically created to foster and support expert learning.[3] We can use UDL to employ the science of learning and motivation to create real-world results.

We're going to need more than just UDL though; we're going to need help. More important, we're going to need partners. We must partner not only with our learners, but also with managers and senior leaders. In building a culture of expert learning, we need to leverage their support to make expert learning the norm, not the exception.

Finally, we will look at how to turn this journey into results. And though the entire path may not be clear all at once, every journey starts with a first step, which is why I will share tools that you can immediately employ to begin the work.

References

[1.] Anne Meyer, et al. *Universal Design for Learning: Theory and Practice*. 1st ed., Wakefield, MA: CAST Professional Publishing, 2014); Peggy A. Ertmer,.and Timothy J. Newby. "The Expert Learner: Strategic, Self-Regulated, and Reflective." *Instructional Science*, 24, no. 1(1996): 1–24.https://doi.org/10.1007/BF00156001.

[2.] Meyer et al.

[3.] Meyer et al.

ONE

LEARNING IN THE MODERN WORLD

Life is flux.

Heraclitus of Ephesus

Change as a constant is an idea that's as old as recorded history, and likely much older than that. Adaptation is the norm. We're built for it; our minds are driven toward discovery. Still, we often act as though maintaining the status quo is somehow our best option. Research has shown that although people from all ages and walks of life admit that many things have changed over their lifetime, they expect the next 5–10 years to be free from any real change.[1] It's as though the idea of more change is too distressing, so we put blinders on and plod ahead, doing things the way we've always done them.

Is it really change that we fear? Would you be afraid if I told you that you'd won the lottery and were about to get a check for $150 million? Sure, you might be anxious about how best to use it, but you'd probably still take the check rather than turn it down and avoid the change. It's the unknown that we really fear. If I make this change, what will happen? Will I fail? Will I lose something valuable? When we can't make an informed cost-benefit analysis of change, we tend to avoid the potential of the worst possible outcome.

This principle also applies to the ways people are used to going about their work. If the strategies and systems for operating have been functional—or at least appear to be functioning—then people and organizations tend to resist changing the status quo unless the evidence is overwhelming that acting in a new way will absolutely create better outcomes.

Then along came 2020, and the world turned upside down. Change had come and could not be ignored. Overnight, all of us in Learning and Development were taking crash courses in Zoom, Articulate, and a host of other tech tools, not only to recreate our in-person training to fit a virtual world, but to support our people to work and collaborate in a virtual space. We had to learn ahead of our learners, with little time and extremely high stakes. This is when it likely became abundantly clear to many of us, as well as to some of our leaders, that we can't keep laying the proverbial tracks in front of the freight train; we had to come up with other ways that organizations could keep up with a rapidly changing landscape.

Prior to the pandemic, organizations were already identifying the accelerating pace of change as a key challenge. Terms like "VUCA"—volatile, uncertain, complex, and ambiguous—began to emerge to describe the challenges of operating in an ever-changing world. Traditional, top-down industrial models of work and learning don't match an economy that is no longer industrial. Unlike in the top-down days of factories and assembly lines, a few leaders at the top, or even a whole L&D department, can't learn for the rest of the organization, and you can't hire all the knowledge needed for every change. A growing number of organizations have realized that the antidote to the challenge of change is learning, learning as individuals, teams, and organizations. They're devoting significant resources to learning—roughly $80 billion per year over the past few years—with a growing emphasis that is less on formalized training away from the workplace and more toward learning on the job.[2] However, throwing more money at the wrong model isn't going to solve the problem. We need to meet our learners where they are, in the modern world of work, where learning looks much different from years past.

Indeed, high-performing individuals and organizations know the truth: Learning is a survival skill. As Satya Nadella, chief executive officer of Microsoft, puts it: "You can't act like a know-it-all; you have to be a learn-it-all."[3] Learning is what enables people to adapt to change and even become drivers of change; after all, innovation is a key factor in the accelerating rate of change, and that innovation comes from learning how to solve new problems or old problems in newer, better ways. Individuals and organizations alike must identify and even anticipate the changes that are going to require new knowledge and skills. People need to learn for themselves, help each other learn, and share knowledge laterally and vertically throughout the organization. Finally, leaders and managers need to listen to their people in order to learn from them about the challenges and potential solutions.

Don't just take my word for it, ask the United States Marine Corps (USMC). They'll tell you that learning is a survival skill. Literally.

The Marine Corps Doctrinal Publications, or MCDPs, codify its culture. They tell every member of the organization what it means to be a marine, including what is expected of them and what they should expect from each other. First published in 1997, the publications cover topics such as warfighting, operations, strategy, tactics, intelligence, and more. Put simply, if you really want to know what marines all are about without actually enlisting, you read the MCDPs.

In February 2020, the USMC published its first new doctrinal publication in nearly two decades: *MCDP 7 – Learning*. MCDP 7 outlines the Marine Corps' learning philosophy, espousing concepts including the need for individual and collective learning at every level of the organization, learning cultures, and learning environments. Why? Because "warfighting is the most complex, challenging, violent, and dynamic endeavor" and the USMC has identified learning as the critical element to develop and maintain the individual and collective versatility and flexibility to succeed "in any situation and at any intensity."[4]

The MCDP 7 tells all marines, from the lowest ranking enlisted member to the commandant of the Marine Corps, that they have a professional responsibility to learn. They must be self-aware and seek improvement. They need to be ready and willing to learn and to understand why they are learning. They need to provide and receive constructive feedback and to learn with the purpose of building professional competence. In short, it is every marine's job to learn.

In the foreword, General D. H. Berger, commandant of the Marine Corps, states: "Continuous learning is essential to maneuver warfare because it enables marines to quickly recognize changing conditions in the battlespace, adapt, and make timely decisions against a thinking enemy.[5] Now, you may not be tasked with improving the fighting capability of thousands of service members, but if you were to translate this quote to your context, it might look like this:

"Continuous learning is essential to organizational success because it enables team members to quickly recognize changing conditions in the marketplace, adapt, and make timely decisions in the face of stiff competition."

Individuals and organizations need to learn in order to survive and thrive in the world of business. It's not enough to hire talent and expertise. Continuous learning is essential in order to keep pace with the accelerating rate of change in the workplace. As learning professionals, we must help people **upskill**: to learn how to improve in their current roles. For example, supporting restaurant waitstaff to use a new point of sale software so that they can be more efficient and precise as they enter orders and process payments. We also support people to **reskill**: to learn to assume new roles. Reskilling allows organizations to retain their people and leverage their skills, experience, and relationships to meet new needs.

Upskilling and reskilling are keys to individual and organizational growth. Recruiting expertise can be much more expensive than developing it internally. A recent study suggests employee turnover can cost approximately one third of a person's salary, say $20,000 for a $60,000 position. However, to reskill that person and keep him or her would cost $10,000—half the cost of turnover. Further, investing in our own people increases engagement, boosting productivity, and further supporting the bottom line.[6] AT&T is one company that has gone all-in on reskilling, investing over a billion dollars in efforts to prepare their existing workforce to meet new challenges. As Bill Blasel, AT&T's senior executive vice president of human resources, says: *"It's important for companies, at the senior level, to engage and retrain workers rather than constantly going to the street to hire."* [7]

Many leaders see the value of developing their own people. According to a 2020 study by PwC, a growing number of CEOs consider upskilling a key to future success; unfortunately, a much smaller number report actually making significant progress in that area. In fact, 1 in 10 of the largest companies have made no progress at all. It seems as though leaders are aware of the challenge and opportunity, but they're struggling to take effective action.[8] So, without the presence of a new approach, many organizations maintain the status quo—top-down training and hiring new talent to fill skill gaps. This is where we, the L&D folks, can be pivotal partners. If we can partner with learners and leaders to develop and sustain a culture of expert learning, we can boost retention, lower overall training costs, and foster innovation. But to help both workers and their organizations make changes, we're going to have to help them change how they perceive, value, and experience learning at work.

Traditional Methods vs. Modern Reality

Let's look at what traditional, pre-pandemic learning has looked like in many organizations and compare it with the needs of the modern workplace. To begin, learning has largely been seen as an add-on, or extra, and has taken place separately from the workspace. During my career, both as someone being trained as well as working in a learning and training department, it often looked like this:

1. Take people out of their workspace and gather them in a large, neutrally colored room (e.g., classroom, conference hall, or hotel meeting space).

2. Give each participant a binder full of handouts and copies of the presentation slides.

3. Present lots of information on PowerPoint slides while talking for long periods.

4. Occasionally, let people talk to each other or write things on chart paper.

5. Break for lunch.

6. Repeat steps 2–3.

7. Ask participants to complete a feedback survey.

Okay, it's not always like that. I've worked with some pretty skilled facilitators and have had the privilege of being trained by a few outstanding people. However, these folks have been the exceptions. Generally, steps 1–7 represent a lot of what's been passed off as supporting learning. It's a top-down, inside-out approach that assumes telling is the same as training or that one method is the best way to teach anything. E-learning is replacing slide-based training as the go-to solution for all things learning. Everything is a video or a module.

While it's true that there is a growing move toward personalized learning, these attempts are largely inside-out approaches, driven by people far removed from the actual work. Learners engage in a digital platform that provides them with a playlist of videos and modules based on an algorithm of their role and past performance. That's certainly more personalized than one-size-fits-all, but as you'll see in chapter 2, real personalized learning means a lot more than an algorithm-driven menu of videos.

These examples represent a content-based approach to learning. In other words, L&D's job has been circumscribed to make enough "stuff" (e.g., slides, handouts, videos, and virtual reality simulations) and hope that the materials meet the learning needs of the organization. I spoke to a seasoned instructional designer, we'll call her Kelly, who works at a global pharmaceutical company, one that has been in existence for more than one hundred years. Kelly told me that she's continuously pushing back against managers asking for what she calls "check-box" solutions, in other words, content-based training that requires her to develop videos or virtual reality simulations, often for problems that aren't really solved through formal training.

Meanwhile, the company leadership is saying yes to every request for new training supports, leaving Kelly and her team scrambling to keep up with the demands. This approach is hampering the performance of both the L&D team as well as the organization at large. She told me, "The trainers are running around with their heads cut off, and really, we're not accomplishing our business strategy right now."

Part of the challenge is the lack of understanding by leaders and managers of how long it takes to develop learning solutions. Each one of these assets Kelly was asked to deliver can take tens, even hundreds of hours to create. One 2017 study found the ratio between development and delivery time was 38:1 for in-person learning.[9] That means it takes an average of 38 hours to create every hour of an in-person workshop. It's 28:1 for live, virtual training, and more than 100 hours for every hour of complex e-learning.

Development time is not the only factor that makes traditional, content-based learning support untenable. As we'll explore more deeply in the next chapter, our modern learners don't have time for lengthy workshops and courses; they need answers now, as they're facing real problems. This is L&D's dilemma: the pace and scope of learning required, particularly in multifaceted organizations, likely exceed our current capacity to design and deliver timely solutions. As legendary venture capitalist and author John Doerr puts it, "Innovation tends to dwell less at the center of an organization than at its edges."[10] So, what are we to do?

"We don't do chase the new and shiny," says Paul Butler, cofounder of Newleaf Training and Development, an organization that eschews the content-based approach.[11] Instead, Newleaf takes what he calls a principle-based approach to learning, supporting people to manage themselves, interact effectively with others, and connect their performance to the greater goals of the organization. They build the capacity of the individuals to improve themselves.

Now, one might think, "Well, those are contractors; they can afford to narrow their focus." However, I would suggest otherwise; they are using a more expansive view of how learning works and the work of supporting learning. Trying to drive learning from the inside out is like playing whack-a-mole, that old arcade game in which a player attempts to hit plastic moles with a cartoon-sized mallet as they pop up intermittently in random locations across a matrix of holes. It's reactive, inefficient, and largely a waste of money (sorry, whack-a-mole fans).

A Partnership Perspective

What if we looked at L&D differently? We're too far from the work to react with sufficient speed and effectiveness. What if we leveraged the people closest to the problems? That's a tactic emerging in companies such as Swisscom, a leading telecommunications company in Switzerland with annual revenues exceeding $12.5 billion. Headquartered outside Bern, it has roughly 19,000 employees. None of them are full-time trainers.

In 2018, Patrick Veenhoff, then head of learning and development at Swisscom, felt the need to create a more rapid, collaborative development model to keep up with the demand and the changes in the workplace. He decided to disrupt the company's more traditional approach to L&D and instituted a supportive, agile approach to training development. The process looks like this:

1. Workers decide they have something to teach others that will help individual and team performance.
2. They take a 45-minute e-learning module created by Veenhoff and his team to teach people to develop their own training.
3. They then develop a draft and bring it to one of the four Swisscom L&D coaches. Working collaboratively with the coach, they refine the training design.

4. The learning experience is offered on the company network.

5. Workers participate and rate the training.

I asked Veenhoff how he ensured the quality and applicability of the training. "I didn't," he responded, "the market did." He explained how they instituted a simple 5-point rating scale, the same used by customers to rate goods on Amazon and other e-commerce sites. Every month, any offering with an average rating less than a 3 was pulled from the menu. The creator then had the option to review the feedback and revise it or abandon it. In this way, he and his team created a learning ecosystem that was self-regulating, collaboratively determining needs and refining practices.

L&D can't know all the problems, let alone deliver all the solutions. We need a different approach. Instead of focusing on building content, let's focus on building capacity and culture. Let's develop and support expert learners: individuals who know how to learn, how to share that learning, and work collaboratively to adapt and innovate. Let's partner with learners and leaders to build a culture that rewards the generation and sharing of knowledge.

Reflect and Connect

Start by getting to know your learners.

- Many organizations rely on leaders and managers to determine what learning is needed, with little or no input from those in the field who are closest to the problems. What about your organization? Who most often decides what must be learned, and how is that determined? Are there opportunities to gain more input from your partners in the field?

- Does your organization have a learning philosophy? If so, how closely does it match what happens in the workplace? If not, would you assume it to be based on how learning is determined, valued, and supported? Write your own learning philosophy and compare it with the explicit or implicit philosophy of your organization.

Resources

- The MCDP 7 – This document serves as both an exemplar of an organizational learning philosophy (more on that in chapter 8) and a primer on learning theory and application. You can download a pdf or audio version for free at https://www.marines.mil/News/Publications/MCPEL/Electronic-Library-Display/Article/2129863/mcdp-7/.

References

1. Quoidback, Jordi, Daniel T. Gilbert, and Timothy D. Wilson, "The End of History Illusion," Science, 339, no. 6115, January 4, 2013, 96–98. https://doi.org/DOI: 10.1126/science.1229294.

2. Fine ATD Research, *2020 State of the Industry: Talent Development Benchmarks and Trends,* (Alexandria, Virginia: Association for Talent Development, 2020), 60.

3. United States Marine Corps, *Marine Corps Doctrinal Publication 7 – Learning,* (Washington, DC: Government Printing Office, 2020). https://grc-usmcu.libguides.com/research-topics/main/usmc-doctrine.

4. United States Marine Corps, *Marine Corps Doctrinal Publication 7,* (Washington, DC: Government Printing Office, 2020.) https://grc-usmcu.libguides.com/research-topics/main/usmc-doctrine.

5. United States Marine Corps, *Marine Corps Doctrinal Publication 7,* (Washington, DC: Government Printing Office, 2020.) https://grc-usmcu.libguides.com/research-topics/main/usmc-doctrine.

6. Work Institute, *2019 Retention Report: Trends, Reasons, & Calls to Action,* Franklin, TN: Work Institute, 2019. workinstitute.com/retentinoreport2019.

7. Caminiti, Susan, "AT&T's $1 Billion Gambit: Retraining Nearly Half Its Workforce for Jobs of the Future," (Englewood Cliffs, NJ: CNBC, 2018), March 13, 2018. https://www.cnbc.com/2018/03/13/atts-1-billion-gambit-retraining-nearly-half-its-workforce.html.

8. PwC Research, *Upskilling: Building Confidence in an Uncertain World: Findings from PwC's 23rd Annual Global CEO Survey.* (London, England: PwC UK, 2020), 26. https://www.pwc.com/gx/en/ceo-survey/2020/trends/pwc-talent-trends-2020.pdf.

9. Defelice, Robyn, *"How Long Does it Take to Develop Training: New Questions and Answers,"* January 13, 2021. Online at https://www.td.org/insights/how-long-does-it-take-to-develop-training-new-question-new-answers

10. Doerr, John, *Measure What Matters: How Google, Bono, and the Gates Foundation Rock the World with OKRs.* (New York, NY: Protfolio/Penguin, 2018), 87.

11. Butler, Paul of Training and Leading at Newleaf, in conversation with the author, September 2, 2021.

TWO

KNOW YOUR LEARNERS

To be an effective, authentic partner to our learners, we need to get to know them—what makes them unique, as well as the common needs they all have. We'll examine how the context of the modern workplace influences the way people approach learning. Along the way, I'll introduce you to Universal Design for Learning, a framework that can help us support individuals through these commonalities.

Understanding our learners allows us to make learning much more personalized, a key ingredient in a strong partnership. Personalized learning means that every learner looks at their learning environment—the content, the delivery, the climate, the tools, the people—and says, "Somebody thought about me when they put this together, and they want me to be successful." Let's start by getting to know the environment in which many people are learning in the modern world of work.

The Modern Learner

According to Josh Bersin, a now-retired partner at Deloitte, the global business consulting firm,[1] modern learners are:

- **Untethered**: Modern learners are increasingly working remotely or in hybrid environments, creating challenges for organizations to effectively support their development.
- **Collaborative**: Modern learners build and use personal and professional networks to keep up with changes in their work and their industries.
- **On-demand**: Modern learners routinely use online courses and search engines to solve problems in real time.
- **Empowered**: Modern learners know they need to continuously improve, and they aren't content to wait for their organizations to support their reskilling and upskilling.
- **Pressed for time**: Modern learners report having less than 1 percent of their

time (24 minutes of a 40-hour week) available on a typical week to devote to training and development.

These traits are symptomatic of the pace and complexity at which learning needs to happen, and some traits, such as being untethered, have increased significantly as people have begun to expect a more flexible approach to their work life. These folks are not having their learning needs met by their organizations, and since those needs aren't going away, these modern learners are finding their own ways to meet them. If modern learners are turning to the internet for information, building their own networks, and going it alone in their upskilling, that means our efforts to support learning in real time, to foster a culture of learning, and to facilitate continuous improvement are not robust or flexible enough.

Though we cannot assume that most learners exhibit these modern traits, these characteristics are helpful guidance because they allow us to anticipate barriers to learning as well as opportunities to leverage strengths. Bersin paints the picture of learners who face barriers of time and distance but also possess some key strengths: they're driven to improve, and they do so by seeking out likely sources of information and partnership. In other words, they're engaging in self-directed learning.

Self-directed learning occurs when learners take initiative to improve their performance, seek out resources, and more or less continually assess their own progress. If you've picked up this book of your own volition, seeking to expand your understanding of teaching and learning and how to improve your practice, then you're being a self-directed learner. Self-direction is a key piece of expert learning, just not the whole puzzle.

Expert learners not only take initiative, they are strategic in selecting the areas where they wish to improve. They can identify, access, and leverage appropriate knowledge and skills. Finally, they learn to create and carry out plans to learn and improve, monitoring their own progress and adjusting plans and efforts as needed to meet the goal in the face of changing conditions.

If we can help all our learners to become experts in how and why they learn, to own their own improvement, to guide their information-seeking and sharing, and to provide clear value and direction in their pursuit of improvement, we can have learning cultures in which individuals, the teams, and the organization all perform better. Barriers to learning and belonging are removed. Everyone wins.

When those barriers remain, people are prevented from acting as their best selves, which hurts them and the organization. Here's why: Learner behavior exists on a continuum, one that is influenced by internal factors, for example, talents, interests, and beliefs and context, such as topic, setting, tools, materials, and more. On one end of the continuum, we have novice learners—ones who are primarily guided by external forces. They learn what they're told, when they're told, for the reasons given to them. This is the type of learner that top-down, one-size-fits-all learning was meant to serve. On the other end, we have expert learners. These are the types of learners we need in the modern world of work (see Table 2.1).

Table 2.1   The Progression from Novice to Self-Directed To Expert Learner

Novice Learners	Self-Directed Learners	Expert Learners
Wait for learning opportunities to be provided to them	Seek out new learning based on interest, utility, and personal growth	Are committed to their improvement and to that of their team, know their own abilities and aspirations, and monitor behavior to optimize effort
Rely on information provided by others	Select information sources and delivery types that best suit their preferences	Intentionally select and vet sources of information, synthesize information from various sources, and draw clear connections to their purpose and their work
Require clear, step-by-step directions for application	Experiment with application, look for opportunities to innovate and optimize, and share ideas and questions with others	Set strategic goals, plan to meet goals and adjust plans based on changing conditions, create conditions that support sustained focus and learning

So, if our learners lack the capacity for expert learning or there are barriers in the environment that inhibit them from operating in that way, we miss the chance to maximize improvement and innovation. However, it's important to understand that a person's learning behavior is not static. We can support novice learners to become experts. Likewise, we can address barriers that can impede the practices of otherwise expert learners, allowing them to operate at their maximum potential.

Learner Variability

It's no secret that today's workforce is more diverse than ever. Technology, globalization, and immigration are connecting people from different places, cultures, ethnicities, and more. Society is placing more emphasis on DEI—diversity, equity, and inclusion. We're examining our systems to pinpoint and correct instances in which one size does not fit all, and in some cases, fits only a select few.

However, the most frequently listed aspects of diversity—culture, gender, language, race, socioeconomic background—affect not only how we're perceived but also how we learn. Moreover, these factors are just the beginning. What many of us have believed instinctively and philosophically—that every person is unique—is now backed by neuroscience. Thanks to machines such as functional magnetic resonance imagers (fMRIs), we now know two fundamental truths about the brain and learning:

- **Learning is variable**. Every brain is unique in the precise way that it engages with learning[2].

- **Variability is plastic**. The way each brain learns changes with experience and context.

Looking at these truths, we are left with two obvious conclusions. The first is that one-size-fits-all approaches to teaching don't work because all brains are different. This makes sense because people have different levels of expertise, different perspectives on learning, and even different levels of confidence in their own ability to learn. They also process information differently, at different speeds, at different levels of complexity, and sometimes through different sensory inputs.

The second conclusion we must face is that we in L&D cannot possibly design for all that variability. We can't design 30 unique learning experiences for 30 different people, especially when we may not even know how they differ. After all, you may not know all, or even any, of your learners. Further, even if you did know them, critical aspects of their variability might not be readily apparent. For example, a study in 2019 found that roughly 30 percent of the professional workforce has a disability, but less than a third disclose that information and usually only then because the disability is physical and hard to hide.[3] This means it's likely that one in five of your learners has a disability and you won't know it.

Laying out all of this visible and invisible variability, we're faced with a quandary. How are we supposed to effectively anticipate and design for infinite variability in order to best support how each person learns? The answer is we can't. That would be like a tailor trying to make clothes that perfectly fit people she's never met, let alone measured. It's impossible, but it's also looking at the challenge in the wrong way.

What if, instead of trying to be tailors, making learning opportunities for people we can't truly know, we created environments where people could tailor the learning to themselves? Just as a tailor knows which dimensions affect fit the most, we can anticipate where variability might significantly affect learning and provide flexibility and support in those areas so that people can make their own adjustments.

But how do we know where variability will most likely affect learning? Fortunately, although our brains are unique, cognitive neuroscience has revealed some common functions of learning that transcend the differences. Understanding these common functions can help us anticipate where variability might play a role in each, shrinking infinite differences down into a manageable array. For the past few decades, the Center for Applied Special Technology (CAST) has been developing, implementing, and refining a framework that will help us intentionally address learner variability.[4] This framework is called Universal Design for Learning.

Universal Design for Learning

Universal Design for Learning (UDL) is specifically intended to foster and support expert learning, the precise skill-set our learners need to thrive in the modern workplace. UDL leverages expansive amounts of research and evidence to translate science into impact. To understand how UDL does this, let's start by looking at how the brain learns. Though no two brains are the same, there are similarities related to the areas engaged in different aspects of learning. We can support learners by understanding what best supports these common aspects and their related brain functions.

The Holy Trinity of Learning

I grew up as a Roman Catholic, and for those familiar with catholicism and other Christian faiths, one of the tenants is the Holy Trinity, meaning that God is simultaneously three separate parts (God the father, Jesus the son, and the Holy Spirit) and one complete being. Each is distinct and has different roles to play, but each undeniably connect to the other two.

Our brains have their own holy trinity when it comes to learning. They have three sets of neural networks that work together, each with a different role to play. The **affective networks** support emotional connection, the *why* of learning. The **recognition networks** govern the intake, processing, and retention of information, the *what* of learning. Finally, the **strategic networks** govern the effective sharing and application of that information, the *how* of learning.[5]

Upon first take, L&D folks may look at these networks and think of a standard flow in a formal training session: get the learners interested (affective), provide them with content to learn (recognition), and then ask them to demonstrate understanding by completing some tasks (strategic). The networks are handing off learning responsibility to each other in sequence, like runners in a relay race passing the baton. Though a natural assumption, the truth is more intricate.

Although we've described these networks individually to help us understand their different roles in learning, they are constantly interacting. For example, to become interested in something (affective), we first need to perceive something that may be interesting (recognition) and decide whether to focus our attention (strategic). We can't think only about emotions at the outset or neglect strategic thinking until the end. Put simply, network interaction is not a relay race, it's a dance. The networks are affecting and reacting to each other. Sure, you may perceive that one network is leading at some point, but they're all in the dance together. Finally, they're always looking for engagement, not just during what others have designated as officially time for learning (workshops, training videos, and so on). These networks are responding to the world in real time.

If we want to help our people become expert learners, we must build their capacity to intentionally connect emotionally, intellectually, and strategically to learning. We also have to create and sustain more effective learning environments, especially those where learning happens most: during work. This way of thinking about how we support our people entails helping them to focus on the *what* of learning. It also entails helping them understand their own emotions and beliefs about their abilities, the *why* of learning. As their partners, we're helping them help themselves to improve by engaging in the *how* of learning, transferring new knowledge and skills into authentic, impactful practice.

Engaging the Three Networks

In his book, *The Happiness Hypothesis*, psychologist Jonathan Haidt compares the challenge of changing behavior to a person riding an elephant.[6] The rider is our logical side, the side that processes and connects information to what we know and to our objectives. The elephant is our emotional side, the one that seeks pleasure, safety, and value. The rider needs to have clear information to figure out where to go, a destination. However, the elephant must also want to go in that direction if they are going to go anywhere. If an elephant, which can weigh several tons, doesn't want to move, no amount of pushing will do. Once both agree on a direction, we also need to give them a clear path, one with minimal obstacles to overcome.

If we in L&D are to change behavior to produce desired business outcomes, logic and information alone can't drive decisions. We need to help our workers foster an emotional connection to what we are asking them to learn. We also need to give the learners something to do with that emotional information. When I design any learning experience, I think about how to help every learner connect emotionally, logically, and strategically with the content. All three networks need to be engaged, and not just initially. It's not enough for learners to connect emotionally at the outset; they'll give up when the learning gets tough. We need to continuously address the rider and the path and address barriers to learning and strategic action.

Universal Design for Learning focuses on engaging the three networks by anticipating where learners might encounter barriers as they seek to connect emotionally, intellectually, and strategically. CAST has developed a set of UDL Guidelines that help us turn all this neuroscience into actionable guidance.[7] We'll explore the UDL Guidelines in more detail in the next chapter, "Know Your Environment," and learn to use them to anticipate barriers to learning in the emotional, intellectual, and physical spaces where the learning is happening.

This brings us to a crucial point to understand about our learners. The barriers to learning are not in them, they are in the environment. Our job is not to fix the people, it is to figure out what's getting in their way and either remove the barrier outright or build our learners' capacity to mitigate the barriers.

Reflect and Connect

- Consider the novice-expert continuum in Table 2.1 on page 17. When have you operated on different levels of the spectrum, and what supported or impeded your capacity to operate at higher levels? Does your workplace learning resemble expert learning and, if so, is it because, or despite, the environment in which you work?

- Learning objectives are often focused on intellectual (*what*) or strategic (*how*) connections to learning. To what extent is *why* called out in your current practice, and how might you increase or extend that emotional connection throughout the duration of the learning?

Resources

- *A New Paradigm for Corporate Training: Learning in the Flow of Work.* In this blog post, noted HR guru Josh Bersin takes us on a brief history of the evolution of training delivery and highlights the needs of modern learners. You can read the post for free at https://joshbersin.com/2018/06/a-new-paradigm-for-corporate-training-learning-in-the-flow-of-work/.

- *UDL and the Learning Brain.* This CAST article, though focused more on traditional educational realms, brings us a simple, clear description of learner variability, the networks of the brain related to learning, and the goal-directed nature of learning. You can access it for free from CAST at https://www.cast.org/products-services/resources/2018/udl-learning-brain-neuroscience.

References

1. Bersin by Deloitte. *Leading in Learning: Building Capabilities to Deliver on Your Business Strategy*. Deloitte, https://www2.deloitte.com/content/dam/Deloitte/global/Documents/HumanCapital/gx-cons-hc-learning-solutions-placemat.pdf.

2. Meyer, Anne, et al. *Universal Design for Learning: Theory and Practice*. 1st ed., CAST Professional Publishing, 2014.

3. Jain-Link, Pooja, and Julia Taylor Kennedy. "Why People Hide Their Disabilities at Work." *Harvard Business Review*, 3 June 2019. hbr.org, https://hbr.org/2019/06/why-people-hide-their-disabilities-at-work.

4. CAST. *Universal Design for Learning Guidelines Version 2.2*. 2018, https://udlguidelines.cast.org/.; Meyer, Anne, et al. *Universal Design for Learning: Theory and Practice*. 1st ed., CAST Professional Publishing, 2014.

5. Meyer, Anne, et al. *Universal Design for Learning: Theory and Practice*. 1st ed., CAST Professional Publishing, 2014; CAST, *Universal Design for Learning Guidelines Version 2.2*. 2018, https://udlguidelines.cast.org/.

6. Haidt, Jonathan. *The Happiness Hypothesis: Ten Ways to Find Happiness and Meaning in Life*. 2006.

7. CAST. *Universal Design for Learning Guidelines Version 2.2*. 2018, https://udlguidelines.cast.org/.

THREE

KNOW YOUR ENVIRONMENT

The learning environment is much more than simply the physical space where learning occurs; it encompasses all the factors that influence instruction, such as methods, resources, technologies, culture, instructors, peers, and the social elements of learning.

Marine Corps Doctrinal Publications 7 – Learning [1]

We just learned a lot about the variability of our learners. Now it's time to turn our attention to the environments in which they learn. Note, I said environments— plural. What we usually focus on is the formal environment, one that was specifically designed and controlled to produce some specific outcomes. Formal environments include in-person and virtual training, an e-learning module, a course, and so forth. These settings have typically been used by L&D professionals to deliver and teach content. However, this approach has been changing.

In the mid-1980s, Bob Eichinger and Mike Lombardo at the Center for Creative Leadership introduced the 70:20:10 model for workplace learning. This model says that 70 percent of learning happens in doing the work, 20 percent comes from social learning, and 10 percent arises from formal learning (i.e., training). Eichinger and Lombardo insist that these percentages are estimates rather than hard-and-fast rules, but the debate continues. Over time, other models that blend formal, social, and on-the-job learning have emerged, citing differing proportions among the three domains. For example, Dan Pontefract, author and head of Learning & Collaboration at TELUS, offers the 3-33 model, with learning coming from one third equal parts of formal, informal, and social learning.[2]

So, who's right? Rather than worry about comparing research and case studies, let's focus on the bigger lesson: Most learning happens as we're doing the work, solving novel problems, refining skills, and collaborating with colleagues. As Elaine Beich stresses in *The Art and Science of Training*, no matter what numbers we use, our job is "to put the learning where the work is."[3] No one disputes that you learn through training; in fact, formal training is often the catalyst for the continued learning that happens when people apply and expand on what they learned. Formal learning has a place; it's just not the only place.

Behavior, the workplace application of the learning, is where we can potentially produce the results we seek. Those behaviors are not happening in a vacuum; they are influencing, and being influenced by, the work environment. Our workplace is a learning ecosystem, a complex of people, their physical environment, and all their relationships within the organization.[4] Those relationships include those between an individual and the senior leaders, management, fellow team members, supporting units, and more.

To make the most of that ecosystem's potential, we need to understand where and how learning happens within it. We also need to understand the systems that are interwoven throughout our organizations and how they can support or impede learning and innovation. From there, we can use the UDL Guidelines to identify and address potential barriers to learning, allowing the ecosystem to thrive. But first, we need to understand where to direct thw UDL lens, and it's not at the people.

Where the Barriers to Learning Live

We can't *make* people learn; we can only set the conditions in which they can learn. We know that people want to learn, so when they aren't learning, or not learning enough or efficiently, we must look at the environment. What's getting in the way, what's missing, and what should be removed? This is our real work: to examine the environment for barriers to emotional, intellectual, and strategic connections to learning.

To begin addressing barriers, we need to come to an agreement about where the barriers live. Barriers live in the environment, not in the people. People are not problems to be solved; they are partners to be supported. Often, when people struggle to improve, we assume, "They would do better if they really wanted to." This assumption lays the blame on the person and suggests that the barrier to learning lies within the person, and it's dead wrong. To paraphrase clinical psychologist and professor Ross Greene, people don't just do well when they want to, they do well when they can.[5] When they can't, it's because something is getting in their way.

You may already look at learning this way. If so, you're ahead of the curve. If you don't, you're not alone, and it's not my intent to reproach you. We tend to approach learning in the ways that we experienced it. So, if our learning experiences—our education, our training, and so on—have told us that when we struggle, it's our fault, then that's how we look at our people.

That's how I used to look at it, and for two reasons, one cultural and one psychological. Culture is, in essence, how we do things "around here," and the earliest formal learning culture we experience is elementary school. In some schools, the culture is one in which teachers can take credit for the success of a student but bear little or no responsibility when a student struggles, even if it's the same kid. Taking responsibility for other people's struggle is scary, so it's avoided.

For example, I remember two events from first grade. The first was when I had a particularly precocious moment in class, writing the word "horizontal" instead of "line" to describe a picture on the board. Ms. Cantlon paraded me around the teachers' lounge, showing me off and preening all the while. Obviously, she had made this possible. I can still remember thinking two things: These people are a lot bigger than I, and I can't believe all these teachers smoke (this was in 1980).

Later that year, however, I earned the moniker "Messball McKenna" because the storage compartment of my school desk was jammed full of papers, old brown paper lunch bags, and other random items. I remember one day vividly—I know exactly where in the room I was sitting and where the same Ms. Cantlon was standing in relation to me when she lambasted me for not being a great organizer at the ripe old age of six. She didn't take any responsibility for this situation; the failure to stay neat and tidy was my fault and if I really wanted to, I would do better. Later, when I was in the U.S. Navy, I spent six months in Nuclear Power School in Orlando, Florida. For 40 hours a week, we studied college-level courses to prepare us to operate and maintain a nuclear propulsion plant. We had weekly exams, and the results were posted for all to see at the back of the training room. If you struggled, you had to spend another 35 hours in the building studying. (The material was classified so all study and work had to happen within the facility.) There was no tutoring, no extra support. You just got punished with less freedom, with the clear implication that you would eventually want to do better and then you would, or you would fail, and it would be your fault. It's no wonder that, at the time I participated in the program, the nuclear power track had a failure rate second only to the SEALs.

Having these experiences and many like them led me to believe that failure to learn is entirely up to the individual. It took me many years, several degrees, and a lot of hard-won experience to shift my thinking. And what made that shift so hard is the second cause—a common fault in human thinking called the fundamental attribution bias. In basic terms, this bias says that when we look at the struggles and missteps of others, we routinely believe that these failures come from something within their personality—they don't care, they're lazy, or they lack intelligence. Meanwhile, when *we* struggle, we look far more at the situation—what environmental factors came into play to cause the challenge.

For example, when someone is late turning in a report, we might assume that the person is disorganized or doesn't care enough to get his or her work in on time. Meanwhile, if we were to be late, we might blame it on conflicting priorities, technical challenges, and other environmental factors outside our control. We didn't want to be late, we just couldn't overcome the barriers in our environment.

Now, one could absolutely argue that there are, indeed, instances when people are, in fact, disorganized, unmotivated, or lacking the knowledge and skill to successfully complete a task. However, that is not the default mode; that's the excuse that lets people charged with performance improvement—in our case, L&D management—get off the hook by blaming the learner and not owning their responsibility for the environment in which the learning is to occur. "I told them: It's up to them to learn."

[handwritten: Leader ... goes both ways?]

At first, ownership of learning barriers can be daunting. We love to take some credit when our learners do well, but we're less inclined to own their struggles. We protect ourselves. If you're like I used to be, you come up with excuses. Then I ran headfirst into a realization, one expertly summed up in this quote from author, leadership expert, and retired SEAL, Jocko Willink: "All your excuses are lies."[7]

That's a hard one to swallow. Admitting that I was lying to myself was scary until I reframed the problem. If the barriers are beyond my control, then I'm powerless to do anything about them, which is hard when I'm being looked at by leadership to produce results. If the barriers were in the environment I was helping to create, then I could do something about them. That responsibility came hand in hand with agency. I can't know everything about every learner, but I can and do know my own designs for learning. So, if I can find the barriers within those designs, then I can remove them or at least provide options for people to overcome them.

Owning barriers is not about reducing learning to a completely externally driven process. That's the problem with the one-size approach; the designer has made all the decisions for the learners, and they are supposed to dutifully follow the singular path determined for them. Learning is something people do rather than something done to them, so this is not about forcing learning into people. Instead, it's about about being better allies to learners by respecting them as individuals in their learning as well as honoring and empowering their ability to make decisions for themselves.

Some folks may not buy the notion that barriers don't exist in people. So, let's address it plainly. I met with some seasoned L&D pros while writing this book, and some—admittedly a distinct minority—put most of the onus on the learner: "I train them. If they don't do it, that's a management problem." That's an abdication of ownership over learner improvement, and it causes people to miss opportunities to better support their people. We'll get into some more necessary mindsets in the next chapter, but for us to begin identifying the barriers, we must be clear: We're addressing barriers in environments, not people. Again, people are not problems to be solved; they're partners to be valued and supported.

Identifying Barriers in the Environment

As we learned in chapter 2, people need an emotional, intellectual, and strategic connection to the learning. So, our work is to examine the environment for elements that would impede those connections. What would prevent the elephant from wanting to move in a certain direction, what would keep the rider from heading that way, and what in that new path presents a barrier to change? There are several ways that you can become familiar with how your learners experience various learning environments. We're going to focus on three:

- seeing the environment for yourself,
- asking people how they experience it, and
- imagining yourself as a learner in the environment.

Then, we're going to look at how UDL can inform and enhance our approach to all three.

Seeing the environment for yourself

A great way to examine an environment is to go to that environment and see it in action. This concept is a hallmark of Taiichi Ono's Toyota production system; it is known as *genchi genbutsu*, which translates literally as "the actual place." However, Toyota defines *genchi genbutsu* as "to go to the source to find the facts to make correct decisions, build consensus, and achieve goals at our best speed."[8] That's what we're doing here.

Go where the learning is happening. Watch what is happening, and what's not happening. What's the emotional climate, the vibe? What's the pace at which information is presenting itself? Is it slow, frenetic, or somewhere in between? Who's doing the work, what are they doing, and what results are they getting? Go at different times, during different activities, and with different learners. Talk to people, ask others what they're seeing, hearing, feeling, and so on. In fact, talk to many people because the barriers may impede some but not others.

Asking people how they experience the learning environment

Enlist diverse people and empower them to communicate their needs, ideas, and challenges when encountering the various learning environments. These **user experts** can tell you exactly what it's like to be them in specific contexts. Locate extreme users, people with the greatest degrees of need related to your problem, allowing you to understand the degree of flexibility and support needed in the eventual design in order to support all your learners. For example, find people with physical impairments, people who have opened up about their learning disabilities, the novices trying to survive among experts, and vice versa. Ask them what's working and what's not. What's getting in the way of them learning and growing? To what extent do they feel like the environment is designed with people like them in mind, and why? These questions can lead to valuable insights, informing your perspective and improving your ability to partner with all of your people.

Imagining yourself as a learner

A journey map (Figure 3.1) depicts the learning experience over time, taking note of the key interactions, or touch points, from start to finish. Journey maps can take many inventive forms, but the most common layout flows left to right along

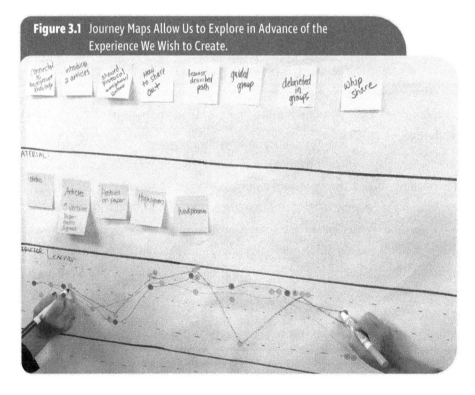

Figure 3.1 Journey Maps Allow Us to Explore in Advance of the Experience We Wish to Create.

a horizontal axis representing the flow of time from one interaction to the next. Creating a journey map should be a collaborative activity, involving at least one user expert, preferably a member of the target audience. Further insight can be gained by involving anyone who has led or supported the environment (e.g., a trainer, facilitator, manager, or coach).

Creating a journey map requires us to determine the aspects of the experience we want to explore, the stages in the process, actions required at each level of engagement, and so forth. These aspects are converted into horizontal rows called swim lanes because of the resemblance of journey maps to a swim race, with separate lanes for individual swimmers to navigate. Together, the actions occurring in the lanes add up to the whole of the race, just as the separate aspects are part of a learning experience.

There is no hard-and-fast rule of what every swim lane should be, but we're likely to find and address barriers and opportunities only in the aspects we map. Let's look at some potential aspects to incorporate into a learner experience journey map that incorporates Universal Design for Learning.

- **Process**: The broad sequence of events from beginning to end

- **Touch points**: Key interactions, including and within sections of the process

- **Emotional state**: Overall levels of positive or negative emotions (Typically, this is relegated to a range of highs and lows.)

- **Thoughts, feelings, and wonderings**: Related to the emotional state, these are common or anticipated learner perceptions. Learner experts

- **Learner Involvement (Active vs. Passive)**: To what extent are learners taking actions to acquire the learning? For example, collaboratively examining and interrogating data and generating interpretations would be a more active level of engagement. Meanwhile, viewing a video or presentation would be a more passive level of involvement. This is not to suggest there should be no passive sections, but continued passive involvement leads to poor engagement over time.

- **Network activations**: How are the different networks involved at this touch point? This can help us pinpoint potential barriers as well as opportunities by examining the functions of learning required at each point in the journey.

- **Scope of the challenge or productive struggle**: Just because we want to reduce friction in the learning experience doesn't mean learning is always meant to be fun. Learning can be messy. Ambiguity can be difficult. However, productive struggle can lead to better learning as well as increased ownership in the learning. The level of challenge should modulate, allowing learners a break before taking on a new problem. Further, needless friction, such as overcomplicated directions, should be eliminated wherever possible.

The UDL Lens

The UDL Guidelines focus on three brain networks—affective, recognition, and strategic—that govern learning, according to neuroscience.[9] The Guidelines serve as a lens through which we can examine any learning environment—formal, informal, social, or on-the-job—to identify barriers to building knowledge and skills. Having identified those barriers, we can plan countermeasures to address them. However, before we look at the Guidelines, I want to make something clear. They are, as I said, a lens; they are not a checklist. That's crucial because at first glance, many folks think they look like one. The point of the Guidelines is not to make sure you provide support or option for every single bullet point. You don't have to provide countermeasures for problems you don't anticipate encountering.

When thinking about the supports and options that my learners may need to address barriers in the environment, I like the term "countermeasures." **Countermeasures** are antidotes to barriers that remain effective only until conditions change or you set a new goal that you wish your learners to meet. I prefer the term countermeasures to solutions because solutions are permanent while countermeasures are contextual, and as we know with variability, context is king. The UDL Guidelines help us strategically deploy countermeasures so that our learners can be successful without putting unnecessary burdens on them or us, their L&D partners.

To begin, we must consider our goals, our learners, and the environment in which the learning will occur. Then, we can ask ourselves some questions:

1. Does the environment include options that can help all learners . . .

    a. make an initial emotional connection to the learning?

    b.   sustain their effort and persist when the learning gets hard?

    c.   own their role in the learning?

2.   Does the environment include options that help all learners . . .

    a.   perceive what needs to be learned?

    b.   process what needs to be learned?

    c.   comprehend and make connections with what needs to be learned?

3.   Does the environment include options that help all learners . . .

    a.   physically access and interact with the content and necessary tools?

    b.   express themselves and problem-solve in authentic, effective ways?

    c.   think strategically to set, meet, and even exceed goals?

Each question focuses on a critical function of learning, engaging an aspect of the trinity. Questions 1a, 1b, and 1c relate to the affective networks; 2a, 2b, and 2c the recognition networks; and 3a, 3b, and 3c the strategic networks. These questions relate not only to the overall environment, but to each learning asset we introduce into that environment. Let's say we're introducing our learners to this whole concept of expert learning, and one of our goals is for our learners to be able to explain the roles of the three networks in learning. One asset we're using to deliver content related to this goal is a short video. We should be looking at how that video relays the information. Is it perceptible to all? For example, is it closed captioned? Does it progress at a reasonable speed, or does it rush through the content? Is it full of jargon or domain-specific vocabulary? Further, we should look at the context in which that video is being delivered. Will the value of the content be easily perceived? Will people readily know what to do with the information contained within? If yes, great. If not, we have more work to do.

The UDL Guidelines, the research-based framework for supporting expert learning, helps us get to "yes" in response to each of these questions. The Guidelines were formulated for, and traditionally applied to, formal learning environments, specifically, the realm of education. However, these Guidelines, as you'll come to learn in the ensuing chapters, leverage sound research and evidence-based practices for supporting learning in any context.

This book translates the Guidelines to the work of learning and development, fostering, sustaining, and continuously improving a culture of learning and performance improvement. Along with the tips and examples within the book proper, I've created an appendix that contextualizes all 29 checkpoints for the world of work.

The UDL Guidelines, as written by David Rose, Anne Meyer, and their colleagues at CAST, allow us to intentionally engage each of the three networks of the brain, translating each into a principle.[10] The **Principle of Engagement** targets the affective network, supporting the learner's emotional connection and commitment to the learning. The **Principle of Representation** focuses on the recognition network, facilitating the acquisition, processing, retention, and connection of new learning to existing knowledge and challenges. Finally, the **Principle of Action and Expression** engages the strategic network, supporting the sharing and application of learning to meet goals and solve real problems.[11]

Each principle is, in turn, divided into three actionable chunks, or **Guidelines**. Let's walk through the flow of each principle and its Guidelines and see how this works. We'll stay high-level for now, digging deeper in the next three chapters.

Engagement

The **Principle of Engagement** focuses on the emotional connection of the learner to the task, in other words, the *why* of learning. If we were to use Haidt's analogy, we'd be speaking to the elephant here. We want to get that elephant connected, committed, and ultimately, owning the learning.

The focus of the first Engagement Guideline, "Provide options for Recruiting Interest," addresses the question "Why start?" That is, how can we foster initial engagement? We can't learn anything if we're not paying attention, so we need to get learners interested in what we want them to learn. Learners will vary in their connection to the learning, but they all need connection. We start by addressing those assumptions. People need to see value and applicability in the learning, and they need to know they'll have some say in how and what they learn. Finally, we need to make learning safe, safe to try, to be wrong, to ask for help, to be their authentic selves.

The next Guideline is "Provide Options for Sustaining Effort and Persistence," which is how we keep the learners engaged when the learning gets challenging. Changing mindsets, shifting behaviors, and developing new solutions to pernicious problems takes a lot of energy. Throw in managing your own behavior, figuring out how to relate to others, dealing with the stress of giving and receiving feedback, and you can see how people are going to need some support to stay motivated. Again, we don't necessarily know in advance who will need support in these areas, but we can definitely count on someone needing help, so we build that help into the environment. We normalize the struggle and the use of support, and we make it okay to need help and to help each other.

The third Engagement Guideline asks us to "Provide Options for Self-Regulation." We help learners examine their own knowledge and skill as well as the effort they have put forth in the learning. Self-regulated learners ask themselves things such as:

- Where's my proficiency now, and where do I want it to be because of this learning?
- What's it going to take for me to close the gap, and am I ready to commit?
- Am I sticking with my commitment, or am I getting distracted or otherwise losing momentum?
- Am I managing my emotions, or are they managing me?

Emotional connection is critical to learning and decision-making. As Haidt describes it, the rider can't push the elephant; the elephant must want to go. Research into the emotional connection to decision-making backs this up. In studies of people with damage to the emotional centers of their brains, researchers found that such people simply cannot make decisions.

Representation

This principle focuses on the *what* of learning, supporting the methods by which the brain takes in information, makes sense of it, and then seeks connection to our prior understanding and our own purposes. The **Principle of Representation** is designed to address common barriers to knowledge acquisition and retention, leveraging over a century's worth of cognitive neuroscience and psychology in the process.

Earlier, I told you that we can learn only that to which we pay attention. Our bodies are always receiving information from light, sound, touch, temperature, smell, motion, balance, and so on. However, our brains can't really process all of that, all the time; they have to prioritize, and that prioritization is what we call attention. Attention filters out most of the information hitting our senses; it's the narrow funnel of data that we let into our consciousness.

The first Guideline of the Principle of Representation, "Provide Options for Perception," focuses on the initial intake of information. If we're paying attention, it must be important, and so we need that information to come to us at a pace and in a format that our brains can handle. There's a reason we don't watch movies at 5x speed. Sure, it would save time, but our brains wouldn't be able to keep up with everything we were hearing and seeing. Likewise, if there's a barrier to sensing, say a visual impairment, for instance, we need an alternative pathway into the brain.

Once we focus our attention and take in the desired information, our brains have to process, or make sense of, that input. The Guideline "Provide Options for Language and Symbols" addresses basic supports for understanding the materials we teach with. These could be subtitles on a video, glossary support for a manual, clear explanations of what certain idioms mean, or how to read a schematic. These supports reduce the friction of learning, making our ability to decipher new information more efficient.

Finally, we come to the third Guideline in this principle, "Provide Options for Comprehension." We process things and store information more easily when we connect it to things we already know, which is all informed by our backgrounds, personal histories, experience, and culture. Our retention, how long we hold on to knowledge and skills, is enhanced by opportunities to use that knowledge and those skills in a realistic application. That application is what we call transfer. Connection, retention, and transfer are mutually reinforcing processes, so the more we can help learners comprehend new information, relate that information to other understanding, and then use this new understanding to actually do something, the more they'll be prepared to actually convert their new learning into improved performance in the workplace.

Action and Expression

The **Principle of Action and Expression** focuses on the strategic network, the *how* of learning. It's the doing part of learning: sharing ideas, experimenting, and building something with our new knowledge and skills.

The first Guideline in this principle is "Provide Options for Physical Action." This suggests the need for flexible tools and spaces and focuses on the physical aspects of doing. To build anything, you need tools, and those tools need to match your physical capabilities. For example, keyboard functionality—the ability to access any function of a digital device using the keyboard—is vital for people who are unable to use a mouse, see a cursor, or otherwise navigate the digital space.[12] Finally, a learning space that doesn't allow for various levels of mobility presents physical barriers to learning; put simply, a tool I can't access is a tool I can't use.

Next, we have "Provide Options for Expression and Communication," which can support creativity and knowledge sharing. Learning is not particularly useful unless it's used and shared, especially when we think about learning as teams and organizations. Therefore, we have to address barriers to innovative thinking, collaborative learning, and the free flow of ideas, both in the interpersonal dynamics as well as in the tools and technology presented for the communication and application of learning. This time, a tool I don't know how to use is one I can't leverage to apply and share my learning.

Finally, we have "Provide Options for Executive Functions." Executive functions are the get-stuff-done processes of our brains. To make the most of them, we have to help learners decide what stuff gets done, develop plans to get it done, locate information and resources necessary to execute the plan, and then put the plan in motion to meet the goal.

Applying the Guidelines

As you can see, there's a lot to unpack from these Guidelines. Over the next few chapters, we will dive deeper into how to help learners connect with the *why*, *what*, and *how* of learning in the workplace. But first, just imagine using these Guidelines, whether in the table form found in the Appendix or as more informal questions found throughout this and subsequent chapters. You can pinpoint aspects of the environment that directly affect learning. Let's take engagement. It's certainly valuable to look for overt signs of emotion in your observations or interviews, but you can go further. Where are these folk identifying, or struggling to find, value and autonomy? What's distracting or threatening? How often, and how well, do they engage in collaboration and feedback? With your journey map, you can examine the elements and interrogate them to see whether they provide the necessary flexibility and support based on the anticipated variability of your audience.

Reflect and Connect

- Consider where we know learning happens, in formal or informal settings and in the flow of work, and compare that with where the emphasis on learning has been in your practice. Is learning being supported wherever learning happens? Are there shifts that can or should be made to better support learning and knowledge sharing across the spectrum?

- Earlier in the chapter, I shared how my variability as a learner was highlighted, both positively and negatively, at a young age. Where has your variability shown up in your learning history? What strengths have you leveraged, and what barriers have you encountered?

- Understanding and implementing UDL requires us to anticipate and address barriers to learning in the environment. To what extent does that align with your current practice? What questions do you still have? Write them down and keep them handy; you'll likely find answers as you progress through this book.

Resources

- *How a Universal Design Mindset Can Support Learning in the Workplace.* In this *Ahead* journal article, Michelle Bartlett and Suzanne Ehrlich discuss how barriers to learning and working can be mitigated through the mindset of Universal Design for Learning. It's one of the first pieces written on UDL in the workplace and I've had the pleasure of conversing with the authors on the topic. I highly recommend you check it out at https://www.ahead.ie/journal/How-a-Universal-Design-Mindset-Can-Support-Learning-in-the-Workplace.

- *The Ten Faces of Innovation* by Tom Kelly with Jonathan Littman. Learn about empathy, human-centered design, and more from the general manager of the world-famous design studio IDEO. Learn more about the book and other resources from IDEO at https://www.ideo.com/post/the-ten-faces-of-innovation.

References

1. Marine Corps Doctrinal Publication 7: Learning. MCDP 7, United States Marine Corps, p. 48, https://grc-usmcu.libguides.com/research-topics/main/usmc-doctrine. Accessed 19 June 2020.

2. Pontefract, Dan. *Flat Army: Creating a Connected and Engaged Organization.* 2016.

3. Beich, Elaine. *The Art and Science of Training.* ATD Press, 2017. p.77

4. "Ecosystem." *Encyclopedia Britannica,* https://www.britannica.com/science/ecosystem. Accessed 29 Sept. 2020.

5. Greene, Ross. *Lost at School: Why Our Kids with Behavioral Challenges Are Falling through the Cracks and How We Can Help Them.* 2nd ed., Scribner, 2014.

6. Fiske, S., and S. Taylor. *Social Cognition.* McGraw-Hill, 1991.

7. Willink, Jocko. "All Your Excuses Are Lies." 31 July 2021. YouTube video, 10:21. https://www.youtube.com/watch?v=zdYVbO5Ie7s

8. "Genchi Genbutsu." *Lean Enterprise Institute,* https://www.lean.org/lexicon-terms/genchi-genbutsu/. Accessed 6 June 2022.

9. CAST, *Universal Design for Learning Guidelines Version 2.2.* 2018, https://udlGuidelines.cast.org/.

10. Meyer, Anne, et al. *Universal Design for Learning: Theory and Practice.* 1st ed., CAST Professional Publishing, 2014.

11. Meyer, Anne, et al. *Universal Design for Learning: Theory and Practice.* 1st ed., CAST Professional Publishing, 2014.; CAST. *UDL & the Learning Brain.* CAST, 2018, http://www.cast.org/products-services/resources/2018/udl-learning-brain-neuroscience.; CAST, *Universal Design for Learning Guidelines Version 2.2.* 2018, https://udlGuidelines.cast.org/.

12. Initiative (WAI), W3C Web Accessibility. "Keyboard Compatibility." *Web Accessibility Initiative (WAI),* 3 June 2022, https://www.w3.org/WAI/perspective-videos/keyboard/.

FOUR

ALIGN YOUR MIND

"People ignore designs that ignore people."
Frank Chimero

Before we go any further into the work of developing and supporting expert learners, we have to make sure we are in the right mindset, or rather mindsets. The intention behind this work is what makes the actual efforts worthwhile; belief is what's going to drive action. The right intention for developing and supporting expert learning is fostered with:

- empathy
- expectations
- ownership

Let's explore each of these considerations.

Empathy

Creating and supporting environments that embrace variability and support expert learning requires empathy, the understanding and sensitivity to the feelings, thoughts, and experiences of others.[1] We need empathy to best know our learners, their goals, their needs, their challenges, and how they will be affected by the context in which they hope to learn. In the last chapter, I shared three strategies: go and see, talk to learners, and map your learning journey, to enhance your capacity for empathy.

Empathy is a core component of design thinking, a methodology to help designers of all types adopt a human-centered approach to solving problems in ways that are desirable, feasible, and economically viable.[2] According to IDEO, leaders in design thinking, taking this human-centered approach is more than a moral question; it's a strategic advantage. "When companies allow a deep emotional understanding of people's needs to inspire them—and transform their work, their teams, and even their organization at large—they unlock the creative capacity for innovation."[3]

You may be familiar with the discipline of user experience (UX) design. That's taking a human-centered approach to new products and services so that they are relevant and meaningful. UX designers anticipate barriers to use and minimize or eliminate them. There's also learning experience (LX) design, the application of design thinking to the facilitation of learning. LXD.org, a leading site for this work, defines LX design as the process of creating learning experiences that enable the learner to achieve the desired learning outcome in a human-centered and goal-oriented way.[4] No matter what we call our efforts to create environments for expert learning, empathy is essential to success.

The environments in which people learn, whether formal, social, or in the flow of work, are emotional, intellectual, and physical spaces that can be designed for optimum learning. Every element, including the messages, the materials, the cleanliness of the space, the temperature of the room, and more, creates the context and the conditions for learning. That's our canvas, and we can create a wonderful scene for all kinds of learners.

Remember that this scene is not for us, but for others, for people who will vary from us and each other, as all people do. The best way to understand what they need is to consider what it's like to be someone other than yourself. As Emi Komawole, editor-in-residence at Stanford's School of Design, summed up this need for empathy: "I can't come up with any new ideas if all I do is exist in my own life."[5]

My Journey to Empathy

I'm not going to lie. Writing this book has been a lot of work, and it's not just the challenge of formulating and organizing the ideas. One of my biggest challenges has been avoiding the assumption that you and I are basically the same. I design, deliver, and enhance individual learning experiences, learning systems, and cultures. So, I could just write this book and assume that it will work for you, too, because you do some or all of that. I could also assume you know the same pop culture references and have a similar sense of humor, allowing me to just have fun with it. That's how I'd do it if I assumed you were just like me. Except you're not. You're you, and that's not only awesome but also supremely important.

My background, as I mentioned briefly in the introduction, is in the public sector. Even though the L&D pros in public and private sectors share the goal of wanting to improve the performance of people, we have differences in missions, pressures, constraints, and so forth. So, I can't write a public sector book and assume it will speak authentically to most of the L&D community. I also have a doctorate degree in education psychology and am practiced in writing for an academic audience. That's not what this book is for, so I can't design this learning experience, which is what I think every writer hopes their work will be, to suit a research journal.

I needed to inform my perspective to better understand who you might be and how to speak to you.

In order to best empathize with you and others reading this book, I've used the same strategies I've suggested. I didn't just rely on my own experiences in learning environments, I went to those supported by colleagues and talked to them about what was working and what might be improved. I talked to a diverse pool of learners, seeking those on the edges of various spectrums, including experts and novices, highly educated and those without any post-high school education, people with physical disabilities, people with learning disabilities, and people from a variety of cultural and ethnic backgrounds. My collaboration with my editor, Billie Fitzpatrick, works very much like a journey map: Where is the reader now? Are we pacing this well? Are we creating enough meaning and value?

Learning is affected not only by barriers in the work environment, but also by the environments our learners might inhabit outside of work. As one L&D pro described, "Sometimes they have barriers that are going on in their own lives and that affects how they learn." People vary in their ability to compartmentalize their work and home life, but even the most adept at doing so can't just shut off their nonwork life during work hours. People need to be their whole selves at work and anticipate that other people may be encountering barriers to learning that we can't see at work.

Empathy Exercise

One thing we can anticipate about learners is that at some point we'll likely be asking them to do something new and unfamiliar. So, it's valuable for us to get in touch with what that feels like. An exercise I recommend trying is a handwriting exercise I picked up from Doug Lipp, L&D veteran and author of *Disney U*.[6] I've used it with hundreds of learners to get them familiar with the thoughts and emotions that can come from trying something new and challenging, and so let's give it a try.

1. Get a piece of paper and a pen.
2. Using your dominant hand, sign your name.
3. Rate the quality of your signature from 1 to 5, with 1 being very poor and being outstanding, with whatever subjective criteria you like to depict excellence.
4. Shift the pen to your nondominant hand and sign your name again.
5. Rate your performance using the same criteria.
6. Reflect on your experience. How did your thoughts, emotions, and behaviors change from the first to the second signature? How did it feel? Did you go slower? Did it require more attention? Were you anxious about how the second signature would come out?

Step 6 is the key to this whole exercise. When I use this tool with learners, I watch for the giggles, the anxious facial expressions, the changes in posture and speed of performance. These are all indicators of their potential discomfort in trying something new. Understanding what it feels like to be asked to do something new and unfamiliar, to be uncertain of your ability to perform well, helps us meet the learners where they may be emotionally as they try to learn on the job.

Expectations

The next key element to aligning your mind to support expert learning is to believe, and expect, that every single person can and will become an expert learner. Clear, high expectations are key, but they're also a challenge because they require us to examine and address beliefs and biases we might have about people.

Studies have repeatedly demonstrated the power of expectations. Put simply, if we believe people can learn, we, as supporters of that learning, are more likely to provide the necessary conditions (feedback, scaffolds, and so on) to support that learning.[7] Conversely, if we don't believe someone can learn, based on their background, role, previous performance, disability, and so forth, we will not put forth the necessary support. After all, why bother doing something we think will ultimately be a waste of our time? In this way, our expectation for our learners becomes a self-fulfilling prophecy. So, to have high expectations for all, let's take a lesson from one of the greatest innovators, and optimists, of the 20th century, Walt Disney.

Walt Disney is famous for many things: movies, theme parks, and a certain mouse. His leadership style has inspired numerous books, articles, and podcast episodes. Disney was known for having very high expectations for his people: If you can dream it, you can do it. More than slogans, he inspired what's known as a "yes, if" attitude. People with a "yes, if" attitude look at every challenge as being possible to meet, given the right conditions and effort.

This "yes, if" attitude has propelled scores of people to progress from entry level positions to the highest levels of leadership. The expectation was that anyone could succeed, including Marty Sklar, who started out writing the employee tabloid at Disneyland and eventually became the president of Walt Disney Imagineering. In a 2009 panel discussion, Sklar stated, "[Walt Disney] knew not to pigeon-hole anyone. You never know what you might find when you give someone an opportunity."[8]

But what if we don't really believe everyone can learn? What if we're more pessimistic about other people's potential, or our own? I've encountered many people in the field, such as managers, trainers, leaders, and more, who think some folks are just born to excel and others just aren't cut out for improvement. According to Stanford psychologist Carol Dweck, this attitude represents a fixed mindset, that is, a belief, that ability, including the ability to learn, is largely static.[9] This belief applies to others as well as to themselves, manifesting itself in a variety of behaviors and thoughts, including:

- **avoiding challenge.** Why do that if I'm never going to be good at it?
- **withholding opportunity.** They're never going to be able to do this, so why should I let them try?
- **low effort.** Success comes from innate talent, not hard work.
- **envy of others' success.** They didn't earn that; they're just born lucky.

This fixed mindset places success and failure largely outside of our control. In a way, it protects us from the blame for failure if we believe we're just not made for some things. However, that protection comes at the cost of agency and opportunity. We deny ourselves, and others, the opportunity to grow and to own improvement. Instead, Dweck urges us to adopt a **growth mindset**, one that sees ability as something that is plastic, or variable, and able to improve.[10]

The growth mindset has science on its side. Numerous studies have revealed the plasticity of our brains. Our brains grow new connections through engaging in deliberate practice, and those connections get stronger with continued, intentional effort.[11] People with growth mindsets embrace challenge because challenge promotes growth. Just as hard workouts, those that exhaust muscles and leave us breathing hard, lead to increased strength and endurance, embracing challenging learning and putting forth significant effort and persistence leads to greater knowledge, skills, and ability. Our mindsets are our self-fulfilling prophecies, succinctly summed up by Henry Ford: "If you think you can or you think you can't, you're right."

The "yes, if" mentality is a growth mindset, meaning yes, this will work *if* the requisite level of effort, time, and resources are expended to make it work. Yes, each and every person in our organizations can become an expert learner *if* we create and sustain the conditions that support that learning. This is the high expectation we should have for others and for ourselves.

These high expectations must come with the understanding that change takes time. Notice how often I mentioned deliberate practice. This shift in thinking is going to take time, effort, intention, and experimentation. Building and supporting expert learning is often described as a marathon, not a sprint. More accurately, it's a journey, not a destination. You're never going to be done, and you have to be ok with that. All great pursuits are like this. I'm never going to be done trying to be a better husband, a better dad, a better person, but that doesn't mean I can't get a little better every day, in every interaction, with every decision.

Through the course of this book, I'm going to walk you through the essential environmental elements of how to partner with both your learners and your leaders. That work is not something anyone, including you, should expect to happen overnight. However, you can get started now even before you finish this book. Then, as you read more and learn more, apply that learning to your practice.

To get you going now, I want to introduce you to the Plus-One approach, something I learned from author, professor, and expert on expert learning in higher education Tom Tobin.[12] The Plus-One approach allows you the opportunity to build your ability to diagnose and address barriers to learning in small increments, building proficiency over time. Here's how it works:

- **Select a learning environment** you've supported before and will do so again. This could be an onboarding seminar, a technical training event, or something else.

- **Determine the biggest pinch point**. Where did the learning get stuck the most? When did the most hands go up or the most energy seem to wane? What did people miss most often on the assessment?

- **Hypothesize the barrier**. What do you think is getting in the way of learning?

- **Design a countermeasure**. What could you introduce into the learning environment, for example, clear instructions, a five-minute break, or visual supports, to address the barrier?

- **Try it out**. Conduct the learning event with the new countermeasure in place. Commit to its use, even if it's causing you some anxiety. This is an experiment.

- **Reflect on the results**. How did the experiment go? Did the countermeasure address the barrier, and how do you know?

The Plus-One approach is about building a deliberate practice through small incremental changes. Don't try to do too much; do just one new thing. In the navy, we had a saying: "Slow is smooth, smooth is fast." Start slowly and build a strong foundation. As your practice becomes more focused, you will become more fluid and more capable and slow will become smooth. You'll find yourself more quickly identifying barriers and having a wider variety of countermeasures that you can deploy to deal with them. That's when smooth becomes fast, and you'll start doing Plus Two, Plus Three, and so on.

The Land of "It Depends"

Let's talk about what some have called the million-dollar question about supporting expert learning through UDL. I've been conducting workshops and delivering conference presentations about UDL and expert learning for years. Without fail, someone will ask, "What does this look like?" The answer comes in two complicated parts. First, what this looks like is variable, dependent on the same factors that influence the learning profiles of your audience: content, context, and plasticity. This variability in application creates an ambiguity that I like to call the Land of "It Depends." Let's revisit goals, barriers, and supports and see how things can change.

1. **Goal**. What is the goal, and what might it look like if people meet the goal? Perhaps you have a goal focused on acquired knowledge. In that sense, UDL might look like providing options for the learners in the ways that they demonstrate what they've learned (e.g., written exam, oral presentation, or artifact creation). However, if each learner needs to develop a particular skill, such as how to draft a professional memo, in that case, he or she needs to demonstrate that skill, but UDL might look like allowing learners to use speech-to-text in lieu of typing.

2. **Barriers**. Where do you anticipate barriers? The barriers may shift based on the goals, the learners, the intended context of the learning, and so forth. For instance, if you are facilitating an in-person workshop, you might anticipate that some people will be reticent to participate in a live group discussion. That barrier doesn't exist in an asynchronous e-learning option, though other barriers can arise specific to that delivery model.

3. **Countermeasures**. Countermeasures are also very contextual. First, varied barriers require varied supports. Implementing supports is an intentional process; you don't need to solve problems you don't have. Second, we can all dream up absolute ideal supports, but you can't rely on pipe dream solutions. All of us are subject to design constraints, such as development time, resources, and location. Finally, your UDL lens will sharpen over time. If I were to observe someone with a lot of practice in UDL, what it looks like for him or her is going to be different from what it might look like for a beginner. While advanced practice examples can be inspiring, they can also be rather intimidating.

All this variability means that UDL can't be used as a plug-and-play, standardized set of strategies. That ambiguity, coupled with initially feeling overwhelmed by the scope and depth of the framework, may make newcomers understandably want someone to shrink the learning to a manageable chunk. "What does it look like?" implies there is a simple answer, a one-size-fits-all example to be replicated.

To be clear, having examples can be very valuable, and that's why you'll find many of them later in this book. However, those examples show what UDL looked like for that content, that context, and that audience. They are examples of what UDL could look like, and that leads us to better questions:

What could UDL look like . . .

for this goal?

with these learners?

in this context?

with these constraints?

within our current capacity?

Reframing the challenge this way opens us up to possibilities and creates agency. We get to decide what UDL is going to look like based on our needs and resources. As our proficiency grows, as content and contexts change, UDL will look different, but we will still follow the same philosophy of firm goals and flexible means and the addressing of barriers in designs, not people.

Ownership

As we explored in chapter 3, barriers live in environments, not people. Once we embrace this framing of the challenge, to figure out what's not working *for* Johnny rather than *in* Johnny, we take ownership of the challenge. We've already discussed how ownership can be intimidating, especially owning the struggles and not just the successes. However, ownership is not just a pathway to agency and impact, it's also a contagion.

When we take ownership of challenges, we are communicating to our learners our commitment to their success. When we point out countermeasures, highlighting how they might be helpful and how to use them, we are providing evidence of our stake in the learning. When we refuse to make excuses, to point fingers, or to use ambiguous word salads to avoid taking responsibility, we are modeling ownership to our learners, our peers, and our leaders.

The more we take ownership, the more we can inspire others to do the same. When we hold ourselves to high standards, admit when we fall short, and demonstrate our commitment to correcting poor performance, we are communicating a culture of high expectations and accountability. The learning matters, improvement matters, and when those things don't happen, someone must own that struggle.

If you are willing to take ownership, don't be surprised when your learners rise to that same challenge. We are partnering with them, which means both L&D and the learners must own the improvement. When we see others take ownership in a challenge in which we ourselves are involved, we are prompted to reflect on our own role in that challenge. Some may call themselves out—"Hey, I think I could have paid better attention"—while others may silently commit to doing whatever they need to do to get a better result in the future. It's not an overnight culture change; it may take repeated evidence of your ownership to build that mindset. But it will happen if you're consistent, transparent, and clear about what you expect of yourself in supporting their performance.

Let me be clear: Taking ownership to inspire others is not manipulation. If you just pretend to own a problem, secretly blaming the learners, and then your people are happy to let you own that problem, you're not likely to continue the pretense. The truth will come out, so be ready to truly own the struggles, and successes, of your learners.

I want to emphasize the need to acknowledge success. I've told you the struggles of the learners are on your shoulders, but don't let any dip in performance dim your perspective of the successes you see. Years ago, I was brought in by a partner organization to facilitate a two-day workshop for 75 people. I thought I was prepared. I'd anticipated barriers, built in supports, and worked my tail off to help anyone I could. But there was one table of five that I just couldn't reach.

Feeling down, I was packing my bag when the workshop sponsor, Kristin, came to me, very excited, saying, "James, this was great."

"Yeah, it was good, but that table over there," I said, nodding my head in the direction of where the five had been sitting (they'd left as soon as we began to close the session), "I just couldn't get them on board."

Kristin smiled and said, "You had 70 people rocking and rolling, excited about this work, for two days. Don't let that one group rain on your parade."

I thought about that for the whole two-hour drive home (Los Angeles traffic is legendary, in a bad way). People, researchers have found, have a negativity bias. We key in on the bad and lose sight of the good.[13] Don't do that to yourself. Acknowledge the areas for improvement, but also pause to take pride in progress. You'll feel better, and you'll take away a more positive view of your learners as well. As French philosopher Voltaire urged us more than two centuries ago, "Don't let the perfect become the enemy of the good."

Reflect and Connect

- Ownership can be empowering, but also daunting. How prepared do you feel to own the barriers your learners face? In what ways are you already exhibiting this ownership, and where might you find opportunities to grow?

- What's your mindset for your own learning, fixed, growth, or somewhere in between? What about your beliefs about others? Is there a difference, and if so, why?

- Earlier in the chapter, I shared how a friend helped me shift my perception of my own performance away from the unbalanced negative. Where has negativity bias shown up in your evaluation of your own performance? The performance of others? What might you add to your practice or the environment to shift that perspective?

Resources

We covered some big ideas—empathy, expectations, and ownership. Here are the resources I used to build on my understanding of these ideas; I hope you'll find them helpful.

- **"What Is Human-Centered Design?"** In a little more than 10 minutes, William Hudson, from the Interaction Design Foundation, will reinforce and deepen your appreciation for the importance of empathy and the need to understand the context in which interactions happen. Though Hudson approaches this conversation through the lens of software design, you can readily adapt his approach to how you begin to design, or redesign, learning environments. You can find it at https://www.youtube.com/watch?v=KkUor_NTuDA.

- *Pygmalion in Management* **by J. Sterling Livingston**. Livingston uses compelling examples from business and literature to illustrate the self-fulfilling prophecy of high (and low) expectations. This article is available online at https://hbr.org/2003/01/pygmalion-in-management. The *Harvard Business Review* allows access to three articles/month for free; after that, you'll need a subscription.

- *Extreme Ownership: How U.S. Navy SEALs Lead and Win* **by Jocko Willink and Leif Babin**. This book has been invaluable to me, and it's probably the book I've gifted the most to colleagues and friends. The authors use real-life examples from both combat and business to illustrate the power and necessity of taking ownership. I particularly like the audiobook version; it's immersive and compelling.

Resources

1. "Empathy." *Merriam-Webster Online*, https://www.merriam-webster.com/dictionary/empathy.

2. IDEO, *What Is Design Thinking?* https://www.ideou.com/blogs/inspiration/what-is-design-thinking. Accessed 1 Aug. 2020.

3. Battarbee, Katja, et al. *Empathy on the Edge: Scaling and Sustaining a Human-Centered Approach in the Evolving Practice of Design.* IDEO, 2014, https://new-ideo-com.s3.amazonaws.com/assets/files/pdfs/news/Empathy_on_the_Edge.pdf. p.1

4. "What Is Learning Experience Design?"

5. IDEO. "Design Kit." *Design Kit: Empathy,* https://www.designkit.org/mindsets/4. Accessed 5 Nov. 2021.

6. Lipp, Doug. *Disney U: How the Disney University Develops the World's Most Engaged, Loyal, and Customer-Centric Employees.* McGraw-Hill Education, 2013.

7. Chang, Jie. "A Case Study of the 'Pygmalion Effect': Teacher Expectations and Student Achievement." *International Education Studies,* vol. 4, no. 1, Jan. 2011, p. p198. DOI. org *(Crossref),* https://doi.org/10.5539/ies.v4n1p198.; Inamori, Takao, and Farhad Analoui. "Beyond Pygmalion Effect: The Role of Managerial Perception." *Journal of Management Development,* vol. 29, no. 4, Apr. 2010, pp. 306–21. DOI.org *(Crossref),* https://doi.org/10.1108/02621711011039132.; Kierein, Nicole M., and Michael A. Gold. "Pygmalion in Work Organizations: A Meta-Analysis." *Journal of Organizational Behavior,* vol. 21, no. 8, 2000, pp. 913–28. *Wiley Online Library,* https://doi.org/10.1002/1099-1379(200012)21:8<913::AID-JOB62>3.0.CO;2-#.

8. Niles, Robert. "Disney Legends Recall Walt Disney and the 'Yes, If....' Way of Management." Theme Park Insider, 2009, https://www.themeparkinsider.com/flume/200911/1551/.

9. Dweck, Carol S. *Mindset.* 2017.

10. Dweck, Carol S. *Mindset.* 2017.

11. Ekman, Rolf, et al. "A Flourishing Brain in the 21st Century: A Scoping Review of the Impact of Developing Good Habits for Mind, Brain, Well-Being, and Learning." *Mind, Brain, and Education,* vol. 16, no. 1, Feb. 2022, pp. 13–23. ERIC, https://doi.org/10.1111/mbe.12305.; Fuchs, Eberhard, and Gabriele Flügge. "Adult Neuroplasticity: More Than 40 Years of Research." *Neural Plasticity,* vol. 2014, 2014, p. 541870. *PubMed Central,* https://doi.org/10.1155/2014/541870.; El-Boustani, Sami, et al. "Locally Coordinated Synaptic Plasticity of Visual Cortex Neurons in Vivo." *Science,* vol. 360, no. 6395, June 2018, pp. 1349–54. DOI. org (Crossref), https://doi.org/10.1126/science.aao0862.; Orenstein, David. "MIT Scientists Discovery Fundamental Rule of Plasticity." MIT News, 22 June 2018, https://news.mit.edu/2018/mit-scientists-discover-fundamental-rule-of-brain-plasticity-0622.; Tovar-Moll, Fernanda, and Roberto Lent. "The Various Forms of Neuroplasticity: Biological Bases of Learning and Teaching." *Prospects: Quarterly Review of Comparative Education,* vol. 46, no. 2, June 2016, pp. 199–213. *ERIC,* https://doi.org/10.1007/s11125-017-9388-7.

12. Tobin, Thomas J., and Kirsten T. Behling. *Reach Everyone, Teach Everyone: Universal Design for Learning in Higher Education.* West Virginia University Press, 2018, https://www.muse.jhu.edu/book/62887.

13. Vaish, Amrisha, et al. "Not All Emotions Are Created Equal: The Negativity Bias in Social-Emotional Development." *Psychological Bulletin,* vol. 134, no. 3, 2008, pp. 383–403. DOI.org *(Crossref),* https://doi.org/10.1037/0033-2909.134.3.383.

FIVE

MAKE AN EMOTIONAL CONNECTION

In the Navy, everyone learns about fire. Fire is the greatest threat aboard a ship, and so understanding fire—how it starts, how it spreads, and how to extinguish it—is fundamental to every sailor's job. And the first thing you learn about fire is the fire triangle: oxygen, heat, and fuel. Fire needs these three things; without any one of them, there is no fire.

Like fire, learning has its own triangle. Earlier, I called it the Holy Trinity: emotional, intellectual, and strategic connection, or as Haidt analogized: the elephant, the rider, and the path. In this chapter, we will focus on engagement, that emotional connection and commitment to learning and the work. And there's no time to lose because engagement is one of the biggest challenges facing organizations today.

According to a 2013 report by the *Harvard Business Review*, "A highly engaged workforce can increase innovation, productivity, and bottom-line performance while reducing costs related to hiring and retention in highly competitive talent markets."[1] Unfortunately, a lot of the news about employee engagement is not good. The 2017 Gallup report *State of the American Workplace* measured engagement in the U.S. to be 33 percent. The good news is that that's high compared with a worldwide average of 15 percent.[2] The bad news is that that means two out of three people view work as almost the opposite of happiness. You might think it's higher in the more advanced economies, but Western Europe measured in at 10 percent. Clearly, we need to do better.

What does engagement mean when it comes to learning, and how do we know when it's happening? Gallup defines **engagement** as being "highly involved and enthusiastic about [the] work and the workplace."[3] Forbes describes engagement as the emotional commitment the employee has to the organization and its goals.[4] Finally, CAST defines engagement as the condition of being interested in, invested in, or motivated toward learning.[5] Synthesizing those definitions, engagement requires an emotional connection, one stemming from interest and a concern about meeting personal and organizational goals, and that connection fuels effort and persistence in the face of challenges. Therefore, to keep things easy, we're going to define engagement to be *the emotional commitment to tackling complex tasks,* be they in a formal learning environment, an informal collaboration, or a work application.

Emotions: Expectations, Value, and Safety

In chapter 2, I laid out the continuum from novice to expert learner. Novices, in short, wait for learning to come to them and then learn only what is required, from the supplied materials, and to the stated purpose. That's not the kind of engagement we really need, so we need to understand the conditions necessary to move from passive, compliant behavior to active, intentional improvement. Universal Design for Learning is, as I said before, based on a vast amount of research into learning and motivation. So, rather than focus on the Guidelines and checkpoints specifically, I want to share the major concepts that shaped them. Don't worry, I've included plenty of examples and strategies of the checkpoints in the appendices, but since fostering expert learning must be intentional, not just a collection of strategies, we need to understand the *why* behind each part of the Guidelines, starting with how to promote an emotional connection to learning.

When faced with a task, learning or not, we ask ourselves three questions: *Can I do this? Do I want to do this?* and, building on that, *What is the price of failure?* The vehemence of the yeses and noes for each dictates whether we'll choose to engage, how much effort we'll put in, and whether we will give up or push on in the face of adversity. Let's look at each one and dig deeper into what we're really asking ourselves.

Can I Do This?

The first question, *Can I do this?* is all about what we expect to happen. If I attempt this task, what is the likelihood of my success? It's a risk assessment based on factors that lie within and outside our control. The first is our estimation of our own ability to complete the task, and is, like so much of what we explore in this book, variable. We don't consider ourselves to have the same ability in all tasks. Instead, we believe we are good at some things and other things might be a struggle.

The second factor is our belief about what lies outside of our control, such as the time and resources available to complete the task as well as the anticipated support or interference of others. If we look at the learning environment and see plenty of support and gauge the time and effort needed to be within our available limits, we're more likely to engage. Conversely, if we're strapped for time and energy, and we don't see anything in the environment that can augment our own capacity, we might not expect much success.

To support high expectations, we first need to clearly communicate them. We are setting a clear bar for each person to meet or exceed. Second, we need to help people believe they can bridge the gap between their current ability and the goal. Remember, learners are variable, so they'll have different perceptions of their own capacity to perform. We can help them take a positive view of their own ability by prompting them to reflect on past successes and showing examples of previous participants' growth and success, as well as by highlighting any opportunities that they will have to leverage their strengths and talents to meet the goal.

We also need to explicitly demonstrate our investment in their meeting those expectations. What are we going to do to help them bridge the gap? We should never hold, let alone communicate, an expectation we don't intend to support. So, explicitly call out what's available to them, from resources, peer collaboration, coaching, dedicated practice time, and so on. The more we can make people feel as though their efforts will be supported and lead to a positive outcome, the more likely they'll be to engage. After all, outside of the lottery, there are scant pursuits in which people have very little expectation of success yet still choose to engage and persist.

Take, for example, the case of Sandro. Sandro is considering taking a certification course in instructional design. He's currently transitioning from being a recruiter but has no formal training in instructional design, so he's a little anxious about taking on the challenge. He's also not sure he's got enough time to balance work, home life, and this reskilling opportunity. However, his manager, Imani, offers to give him three hours per week during work time to study for the certification course. She also offers to pair him with a mentor, a seasoned instructional designer who can help him make the shift. With this support, Sandro knows he can complete the course successfully.

Do I Want to Do This?

The lottery example highlights the second factor, *why* the task is worth doing, which brings us to our second question: *Do I want to do this?* You may have heard the saying, probably from someone in marketing, that everyone listens to WII FM. If so, you know they're not actually talking about radio. WII FM stands for "What's in it for me?" It's a question of value, the *why* of the learning, and that value is individual. After all, it's what's in it for *me*. However, although perception of value is variable, it's based on a mixture of four factors: importance, interest, utility, and cost.

- **Importance**. How important is this to me? How important is this to the organization? To society? Is there prestige or high regard associated with completing this successfully? Important tasks often engender some respect or recognition from their completion.

- **Interest**. We do all kinds of things because they're interesting and fun— things that stimulate our curiosity, emotions, and imaginations. However, we don't all find the same things to be fun and interesting; there's that variability again, and the degree of interest in tasks change.

- **Utility**. When looking for utility value, we ask, Can I use this to accomplish something I want to do? Likewise, when someone asks, When am I ever going to use this? they are telling you that there's a barrier to them perceiving the utility value.

- **Cost**. Cost represents our estimation of what we have to give up in order to engage:

    ○ How much time, energy, and resources is it going to take to get this done?

    ○ What could I be doing instead?

We can speak to the value of learning in many ways: examples of past successes and the benefits of those successes, the importance to the team performance, and so forth, but as partners to our people, we can also prompt them to identify the value for themselves. How might this help you? Where would you use this? What would your work look like if you gained this new knowledge and skill? This prompts the learner to identify themselves within the context of the learning, to find their own answers to "What's in it for me?"

What Is the Price of Failure?

Our expectation of success and the value that can come from it are, in our minds, weighed against the price of failure. If I fail, what happens? Do I get penalized? Or is the emphasis on learning, not performance? Do others think less of me, or are we in a mutually supportive environment? Is the emotional payoff worth the investment and the risk? The challenge for L&D is to frame tasks in ways that promote positive answers to those questions. Defining the price of failure brings us to one of the most important factors in successful individual, team, and organizational learning and performance: psychological safety.

Psychological Safety

We are happier when we are learning. This is true on a chemical level; when we are actively searching out novelty, like exploring new material, testing out new equipment, or even checking our phones for alerts, our brains release dopamine. It's a reward for the act of exploring or acting upon interest. *Seeking* is an inherent biological function that's helped drive humans to gain new information, cover new ground, and continuously evolve.

The biggest impediment to seeking is fear. When we are afraid, our impulse is not to discover new things but to stick to the familiar in hopes of removing the condition of being afraid. Many factors can make us afraid at work: job insecurity, rebuke from colleagues, or even challenges to our perceived competence at a particular task. Fear kills learning, so we must create and sustain an environment of **psychological safety**, where candor and vulnerability are welcome and where the emphasis is on learning and growth, not perfection and blind obedience.[6]

How do we make learning safe? We anticipate potential threats. Where might someone find the experience stressful or unsafe? Are we asking people to try something completely new? Are they to perform a complex task in front of an audience, perhaps their manager? Do we have novices who may fear judgment from their expert peers for not having the same level of knowledge and skill? All these questions and more can come into play, and we may not know beforehand who may be afraid or why. But we can do some things to make it safe for all learners.

First, we can explicitly declare the environment to be one where learning, not perfection, is the expectation. This may seem simple, but giving explicit permission tells the learners that they should not judge themselves or others harshly for asking questions, requesting assistance, offering ideas, or hazarding guesses. Guesses should not be hazards; they are opportunities to learn. Innovation does not occur in a do-it-right-the-first-time-or-else environment.

Second, we can make clear the supports—what they are, where they are, and how to access them independently, without asking special permission. Show everyone where knowledge banks, tools, and other resources might be found. Outline the acceptable coping skills, for example, let people know it's okay to take breaks if needed or to get up and stretch. This type of freedom may challenge the perceptions of some about what learning looks like.

Finally, we can model this safe-to-try environment. Often, when working with a group in a workshop setting, I like to declare to the group that I am likely going to make the most mistakes out of anyone in the room, they'll be the most public, and that I'm okay with that because their learning is what's important and I am relying on their good graces and cooperation to work through any mistakes and help them meet their goals.

I also make it clear that I expect questions; instead of asking, "Who has a question?" I instead ask, "Who's going to be the first to ask me a question?" This tells the learners that I don't expect them to absorb everything immediately or to just blindly accept content we're exploring. This works not only in workshops but also in team meetings, in which power and knowledge variances can make it intimidating to ask a question.

UDL CONNECTION

The first Guideline in the **Principle of Engagement**, "Provide Options for Recruiting Interest," is grounded in the concepts of expectations, value, and safety. Here are the three checkpoints in that Guideline, followed by questions based on each. You can use these to pinpoint barriers in the learning environment.

"Provide Options for Recruiting Interest"

- Provide options for individual choice and autonomy.
  - To what extent can learners make decisions about how best to approach the learning and play to their strengths, interests, and preferences?
- Provide options for relevance, value, and authenticity.
  - To what extent can learners readily identify why the learning is worth their time and effort?
- Minimize threats and distractions.
  - To what extent is the learning environment a safe place to engage and experiment, and can learners readily focus on the learning?

You can learn more about this Guideline and its checkpoints in appendix A.

Building on the Foundation

What does engagement, that emotional connection, look like? Is it working continuously, following directions, looking at the presenter? Researchers often measure motivation through three indicators: active choice, effort, and persistence.[7] Active choice is the extent to which the learner chooses to engage. Promoting active choice is the work we just explored: setting expectations, promoting value, and making the learning environment safe. To then coax learners to give strong effort and persist through challenges, we must carefully build on that foundation. We've all experienced the dip in motivation that can come from changing conditions, such as encountering unexpected challenges, distractions, diminished perceptions of value, or emerging threats to safety. These are barriers that can decrease or even extinguish our emotional connection, so let's look at how we can shape the environment to deal with those barriers.

Let's start with expectations. It's one thing to expect success before you start the work, but what about once you're doing it? How do you know you're being successful, and is your reality matching what you anticipated when you started? As we do something, we are continuously updating our perception of that task. Remember, people are thinking about their likelihood of success, of bridging the gap between their current capacity and the goal. To keep their momentum going, we need to continuously inform their expectations and also make clear that they have support to meet their goals.

Give Feedback

Feedback is a key driver of performance. Whether you're driving a car, writing a report, or designing new software, you need feedback to gauge the effectiveness of your efforts. Feedback loops are continuous cycles of information that use current performance to guide future performance. For example, we use speedometers to monitor and adjust how fast we drive, looking at our current speed and increasing, decreasing, or maintaining as needed.

Feedback comes in two varieties: extrinsic (from outside sources) and intrinsic (from within us). Both are important to individual and team performance. I need to monitor my own behavior to make sure I'm doing my part so that I get something from the learning and so I help the team to accomplish the goal. I also need to provide feedback to my teammates so that we can work better together. Finally, I need to receive feedback so that I can benefit from diverse perspectives on my performance.

Feedback is most effective when it is:

- **Specific**: If we want people to improve in their performance, we need to do more than tell them, "You've got to do better." Target specific behaviors and their impact on performance.

- **Timely**: Feedback is best delivered when the performance is fresh in the minds of both the recipient and the provider of the feedback. This allows people to make changes immediately rather than continue to perform without the necessary guidance. Further, the longer the delay in feedback delivery, the harder it is for the recipient to remember the actual details of the performance (what they did, when they did it, and why).

- **Actionable**: Describe what improvement looks like and the specific actions the recipient can take to reach that new level of performance.

Feedback is tricky; we must consider both the content (what we are going to say) and the manner (how we are going to say it). Starting with the content, begin by focusing on a point of competence and how that could be enhanced. We can, when needed, address deficits in performance, but we should avoid the trap of focusing solely on the negative, which can lower self-efficacy and even lead to resentment.

For the manner of feedback, remember the end goal is to improve performance, so it's important that the recipient can process the feedback without being thrown off by the delivery. Also, remember variability: people will differ in their receptiveness based on their beliefs about the source, the context of the delivery (when, who is present, and so on), and the method (email, handwritten note, or public acknowledgement).

Finally, feedback should prompt rather than preempt critical thinking. Consider asking questions that lead to the learner's discovery of the necessary information and next steps. Promoting self-assessment and **metacognition**, thinking about one's thinking, can support greater ownership of performance and support the foundation of the highest level of emotional connection, self-regulation, which we will explore later in this chapter.

Learn in Teams

Having one or more partners in accomplishing a task, particularly a challenging one, can lead to increased expectations of success because it means we're not alone in the work. We can divide and conquer, share ideas and questions, and provide each other with valuable feedback.

However, it's more complicated than just sitting several people together and telling them to work together. Research shows that there are some key elements that affect the effectiveness of collaboration, and they echo much of what we're exploring in this Guideline. They include:

- **Having clear, mutually agreed upon goals**. Each member must understand and embrace the end game of the learning to maximize his or her individual contribution. You can support this by either providing group goals or facilitating group goal setting.

- **Crafting and Coordinating Plans**. All members of the group need to be clear about their role in the learning. You can support teams to set clear expectations and to generate plans by providing planning tools and exemplars they can use as references to guide their efforts.

- **Regulating self and peer performance through feedback**. Internal and external feedback loops are required to keep people on track and, when necessary, to adjust to changing conditions.[8] You can support this by modeling the delivery and reception of feedback, by explicitly calling out the characteristics of good feedback, and providing tools and processes that guide people to provide and receive feedback from each other.

- **Reflecting on team performance**. Acknowledging the progress of the team allows each member to see the impact of their collective efforts, fueling further engagement. You can support this by providing the necessary time, guidance, and data for this reflection.

- **Incentivize knowledge-sharing over knowledge-hoarding**. One of the biggest barriers to knowledge-sharing is anxiety that sharing will rob individuals of opportunities for reward and even threaten their job security. If I give away all my knowledge, what will they need me for? If ideas are to be shared freely, we need to incentivize people to do so and make clear that sharing key insights will not diminish their individual value to the team.

By developing capacity to learn in teams, you're helping to build and sustain a culture in which learners can share ideas, make meaningful contributions to the improvement of others, and incentivize collaboration over knowledge-hoarding.

Reinforce Value

Team learning and feedback can reinforce our expectations of success, but that doesn't mean that meeting challenging expectations will be easy; if it did, we'd have to reexamine our definition of challenging. When the work gets hard, learners need to stay connected to the *why*, to feel that their giving significant effort and persisting through challenges will still be worthwhile. For teams, some of that value will be derived by the intrinsic reward that comes from interacting with and helping others. Regardless, as partners, we can do more to reinforce the value of the work.

We can:

- **revisit the goal** and its relation to the work, both as individuals and teams ("Remember, we're doing this because . . ."). These reminders of the goals can be delivered within the learning, highlighting the learning during routine meetings, and more.

- **prompt reflection**. ("Think about how this is going to help you when . . .").

- **create a line of sight to the end game**. Bring in examples of the end game, creating a clear connection between the learning and a positive result. Share stories and comments from end users who have been positively affected by past successes in this hard work.

- **highlight the ancillary benefits of the learning**. They're learning not just new technical knowledge and skills, but also *how to learn,* as individuals and teams. They can leverage that ability in both their work as well as their personal lives.

We can be effective partners to our people by continuously reinforcing the *why* so that the learning matters to all of us, not just the organization.

Keeping It Safe

Earlier, I mentioned research on effective teams and the importance of psychological safety. In a two-year study of its employees, Google found that psychological safety was far and away the biggest driver of successful teams.[9] Working with others and sharing our ideas and challenges requires us to be vulnerable. Vulnerability, when treated with respect and dignity by others, leads to trust. However, vulnerability that is exploited deters people from ever being open in the future.

This goes not only for the person who is being vulnerable, but for those witnessing such vulnerability. People are social learners; we observe the behaviors of others and take notes for our own behavior. When we see someone open up about challenges and seek help, and then, if that openness is met with a response of support and respect, it makes it easier for us to also be vulnerable and to see others as individuals. The trust can spread because we can grow to imagine ourselves being that vulnerable and to treat others the way we'd want to be treated. However, if that vulnerability is met with scorn, or even just ambivalence, we're much more likely to retreat to the novice learner behavior—just tell me what to do—or even disengage altogether.

We can cultivate that psychological safety in several ways. First, we can emphasize growth and iteration over perfection. Remember our mindset: It's about continuous improvement and deliberate practice, not about getting it right the first time. Solicit learners' feedback on your support of their learning. I frequently tell learners how many iterations a learning event has gone through and how I want their insights to make it better for the next group.

Model vulnerability. Admit when you make a mistake and need help and allow others the opportunity to respond with the grace and support they'd want for themselves.

Spotlight experimentation and the learning that can come from it even if the experiment itself is a failure. We want what Duke University professor Sim Sitkin calls **intelligent failures**, the missteps that come from an iterative pursuit of novel solutions.[10] In this way, an iterative approach, which includes small failures, can inform and reinforce learning. If we are careful to observe changes and make thoughtful attributions to the correlating impact on results, the process of iteration can help sustain and even increase engagement.

Our learners are variable when it comes to their mindsets around failure. Some will likely be ready for anything, while others may be more risk averse. We can't assume everyone is ready for experimentation. We'll need to set the conditions that say, "Failure is ok if you learn from it." That's key: We're not saying all failures are equal; we don't want mistakes that come from inattention or recklessness. What we do want is the readiness to grow in new ways, and that means trying things that aren't guaranteed to go right the first time.

UDL CONNECTION

The next Guideline in the Principle of Engagement is "Provide Options to Support Effort and Persistence." You'll see how all we just covered—feedback, safety, value, expectations, and collaboration—are supported by the four checkpoints.

"Provide Options to Support Effort and Persistence"
- Heighten salience of goals and objectives.
  - To what extent are learners reminded why the learning is worth the work?
- Vary demands and resources to optimize challenge.
  - To what extent are learners challenged in ways that optimize, rather than inhibit, their engagement?
- Foster collaboration and community.
  - To what extent do learners have the opportunity and support to learn collaboratively?
- Increase mastery-oriented feedback.
  - To what extent can learners get data that inform their perception of their performance?

In addition to these checkpoints and related questions, L&D may also want to inquire about the culture of psychological safety and continuous improvement, asking:
- To what extent are learners supported to take risks and learn from mistakes?

You can learn more about this Guideline and its checkpoints in appendix A.

Empower your people

Expert learning requires more than effort and persistence; it requires an understanding of the learners' own role in their successes and struggles. As I described in chapter 2, expert learners take ownership of their learning; they are committed to their improvement and to that of their teams. They are aware of their current ability, they push themselves for continuous improvement, and they monitor their behaviors to optimize efforts. In the words of psychologist Barry Zimmerman, they engage in self-regulation.[11]

Self-regulation is a cycle of setting goals, monitoring progress toward those goals, and then reflecting on performance.[12] Each stage of the cycle informs the next. Self-regulated people have enough awareness of their own knowledge and capacity that they can: assess their current levels of ability; set goals; strategize the pursuit of those goals; and, upon completing a task, assess their own performance and new level of capability. In short, self-regulation is knowing and owning your role in the process of actualization.

We'd like to assume this is how everyone approaches learning and work, but like so many things, our ability to self-regulate is variable and dynamic. We vary in our sense of agency, based on experience, personality, and context. **Meetacognition**—the thinking about our own thinking[13] – also comes into play. If we don't have the capacity to objectively measure our ability, we can become ignorant of our need to improve or blind to our strengths, both of which discourage us from improvement. Finally, learning can be stressful, and we vary in our capacity to cope with stress. We also vary in the cumulative stress in our lives. Each of these variables means some folks are going to need more flexibility and support to ensure they don't get overwhelmed.

We can support our people to be self-regulating learners both by building their capacity to engage in the process as well as by creating the conditions that support that process. Let's go through each phase and see how we can be supportive partners in their expert learning.

Self-Regulated Learning (SRL)

Psychologist Barry Zimmerman pioneered the study of self-regulated learning. As we've seen, work is learning, and so, as we seek to build people's capacity to effectively and continuously improve, we can benefit by effectively applying his research in this area.

Zimmerman describes self-regulation as a 3-stage cycle:

1. Forethought: How can I improve?
2. Performance control: Am I behaving in ways that will lead to improvement?
3. Self-reflection: Did I make the improvements I sought? Why or why not?

Though Zimmerman's work has largely been applied to formal learning environments, recent research by the trio of Anne Kittel, Rebecca Kunz, and Tina Seufert supports building worker capacity to self-regulate as part of a strong learning culture.

To go deeper into the application of SRL at work, check out this article from *Frontiers in Psychology*: https://www.frontiersin.org/articles/10.3389/fpsyg.2021.643748/full.

Where am I, and where do I want to go?

As we just discussed, the first part of self-regulation requires understanding our current capacity. What is my current level of knowledge and skill, and how do I know? Some people overestimate their level of knowledge and skill in a particular area, leading to lower motivation to improve; this is known as the Dunning-Kruger effect, and it is a leading cause of mediocre performance. Meanwhile, others suffer from impostor syndrome: They don't give themselves enough credit for the knowledge and skills they have, lowering their expectations for their own growth. Figure 5.1 lays out the challenges of understanding our true level of competence.

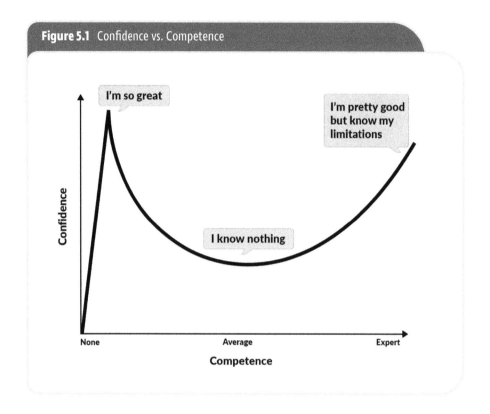

Figure 5.1 Confidence vs. Competence

People who overestimate their ability find themselves on the left part of the curve near what's known as the Peak of Mt. Stupid.[14] Those who underestimate themselves, having impostor syndrome, show up on the right-hand side but significantly below the curve. These people don't give themselves enough credit for what they do know. The remedy for both is objective measures of competence.

We can help learners see what real knowledge and skill looks like and allow them to gauge their performance against that reference point. We can provide them with tools to self-assess their ability, for example practice exercises and quality indicators. Working in teams can provide them with peers of similar ability who can support their growth and allow them to support others. Train them in metacognitive strategies, such as self-explanation, or the Feynman technique, which, in part, requires them to explain their new knowledge in the simplest possible terms, as though speaking to a small child. Richard Feynman, a Nobel prize-winning physicist, encapsulated his learning technique in four simple steps:

1. Identify the subject.
2. Explain it briefly and plainly.
3. Identify your knowledge gaps.
4. Organize, simplify, and tell a story.[15]

The more learners understand where they are, the better they can set expectations for realistic, meaningful growth. Whenever possible, we should be building off their previous performance, allowing them to reflect on how they've been able to meet or exceed expectations. Challenge them to go even further and ask them to assess their next opportunity for growth.

Consider individual performance plans and the processes related to them. Ideally, learners and their leaders should be co-constructing these plans in a way that allows learners to have some autonomy in their improvement as well as to develop clear connections between their goals and those of their team, department, and organization. These plans should also detail the support the individuals will receive in their pursuit of their improvement.

Further, we can teach and support learners to engage in self-regulation strategies before any learning event, using three simple questions that prompt them to set intentions and success criteria:

- What am I learning?
- Why am I learning this?
- How will I know I have learned it?[16]

Owning the learning behaviors

Next in the cycle of self-regulation is the *performance control* phase—the monitoring of one's own learning and behaviors. We can anticipate challenges in areas such as staying on task, persisting through challenges, and self-reflection; let's be proactive in our partnership with people so they can deal with any barriers they may encounter.

Again, if they have performance plans, they need to own their role in meeting those plans. Encouraging learners to set behavioral goals for improvement—deciding what they're going to do, or not do, to meet their goals—is a great way to increase engagement because it makes learners mindful of their role in their success.

We can support learners to set behavioral goals by helping them determine what it's going to take in time, effort, and persistence to meet the goals. With that estimate developed, then anticipate barriers and help the learners identify strategies and supports to mitigate them. For example, let's say Alex has first determined that he will devote five hours per week to completing an online certification in project management. He then asks, "How realistic is five hours a week over the next few months?" Looking ahead, Alex then identifies the close of the quarter as being an especially busy time, making five hours a week seem much more of a lift than at present. He then begins strategizing how he might frontload a few more hours before that time as well as ways to optimize his schedule to create a bit more room during the busy period.

We've come to the third phase of self-regulation: self-reflection. This is when the learner asks, "Did I meet the goal? If I did or did not, why? What did I do, or not do, that led to my outcome? What worked, what didn't, and how can that information help me set and achieve my next goal?" These are the questions that inform this reflection, and we can support learners to be reflective until they are ready to initiate that reflection on their own.

Some possible reflective prompts include:

Where am I showing improvement? What did I do to make that happen?

- Where do I still have gaps in my knowledge and skill? What can I do to fill those gaps?
- What did I do today that didn't work as well as I'd anticipated?
- Am I giving my best effort? Why or why not?
- What knowledge and skills do I now have that I can share and use to help the team?

Self-reflection questions such as these enable the learners to examine their outcomes, but even more important, they can examine the factors that led to those outcomes and their relative control over those factors. If we want to build empowered, expert learners, they need to believe in themselves and know that they can drive their own learning. Learning is something they do for themselves, not something done to them by others.

Agency is one of the key elements of continuous learning; however, agency alone is not enough. Remember what we've learned about expectations and value. Agency must be paired with support as well as with perceptions of value. If people have challenges identifying supports or think that the learning won't lead to benefits that justify the costs (time, effort, or missing out on other activities), then we need to address those barriers in the environment.

***

Over the course of this chapter, we've learned the foundational elements necessary for purposeful, motivated learning: expectations, value, and safety. Our work as partners with learners is two-fold. First, we build their capacity to identify value, set high expectations for themselves and identify supports to help them meet them, and ultimately to have the skills of self-regulating, continuous learners. Second, we have to create and sustain environments that allow for those skills to be applied. Even people who have operated like expert learners can be reduced to novice behavior if there are significant barriers to expectations, value, or safety.

UDL CONNECTION

The final Guideline in the **Principle of Engagement**, "Provide Options for Self-Regulation," supports that cyclical process. Here are the three checkpoints in that Guideline, followed by questions based on each, to help you support your learners to own their improvement.

Provide Options for Self-Regulation
- Promote expectations and beliefs that optimize motivation.
  - To what extent do all learners expect to improve and find meaningful value in improvement?
- Facilitate personal coping skills and strategies.
  - To what extent can learners readily identify and engage in behaviors that will support their learning and the learning of others?
- Develop self-assessment and reflection.
  - To what extent can all learners pause and reflect on both their performance and their role in achieving it?

You can learn more about this Guideline and its checkpoints in appendix A.

Reflect and Connect

- In thinking about the learning environments you currently support (e.g., formal training, e-learning, and coaching), How psychologically safe are those environments? What threats exist, and where have you made efforts to mitigate them? How might you "Plus One," that is, add one change that might further enhance the safety and allow learners to focus on the learning rather than on the threats?

- At this point in the book, where is the value in what you've learned so far? Interest? Utility? Importance? A mix? Has that value math changed as you've progressed, and, if so, what do you think shifted your perspective?

- Reflection is a key component of self-regulation. Besides answering these questions, how have you built reflection into your learning process? How do or might you support others to reflect on their learning?

Resources

If you want to go deeper into the science of motivation and engagement, I recommend the following works. These are not paid advertisements; they are some of the resources I have used to deepen my own understanding of how to move the elephant.

1. *Switch* **by Chip and Dan Heath**. This excellent work combines a host of psychological research as well as real-world case studies to illustrate the power of engaging people in both heart and mind and then providing some clear direction to make real change.

2. *Drive: The Surprising Truth About What Motivates Us* **by Daniel Pink**. Counter to suggesting traditional carrot-and-stick approaches to motivation, Pink urges us to support our people through autonomy, mastery, and purpose.

3. *Alive at Work: The Neuroscience of Helping Your People Love What They Do* **by Dan Cable**. Cable takes us through a biological approach to boosting engagement by making work safe, allowing people to bring their whole

selves for work, making room for creativity and experimentation, and connecting with a compelling purpose.

4. For more on the Feynman technique, read https://medium.com/taking-note/learning-from-the-feynman-technique-5373014ad230 or check out the video "How to Learn Faster with the Feynman Technique" by Thomas Frank at https://youtu.be/_f-qkGJBPts.

Resources

1. Harvard Business Review. *The Impact of Employee Engagement on Performance - SPONSOR CONTENT FROM ACHIEVERS*. Harvard Business Review, 2013. hbr.org, https://hbr.org/sponsored/2016/04/the-impact-of-employee-engagement-on-performance.

2. *State of the Global Workplace*. 1st edition, Gallup Press, 2017.

3. *State of the American Workplace*. 1st Edition, Gallup Press, 2017.

4. Kruse, Kevin. "What Is Employee Engagement?" *Forbes.Com*, 22 June 2012, https://www.forbes.com/sites/kevinkruse/2012/06/22/employee-engagement-what-and-why/#6507480d7f37.

5. Meyer, Anne, et al. *Universal Design for Learning: Theory and Practice*. 1st ed., CAST Professional Publishing, 2014.

6. Edmondson, Amy. "Psychological Safety and Learning Behavior in Work Teams." *Administrative Science Quarterly*, vol. 44, no. 2, June 1999, p. 350. *DOI.org (Crossref)*, https://doi.org/10.2307/2666999. Edmondson, Amy C., and Per Hugander. "4 Steps to Boost Psychological Safety at Your Workplace." *Harvard Business Review*, 22 June 2021. *hbr.org*, https://hbr.org/2021/06/4-steps-to-boost-psychological-safety-at-your-workplace.

7. Schunk, Dale H., et al. *Motivation in Education: Theory, Research, and Applications*. Pearson, 2014., p.5

8. Phielix, Chris, et al. "Awareness of Group Performance in a CSCL-Environment: Effects of Peer Feedback and Reflection." *Computers in Human Behavior*, vol. 26, no. 2, Mar. 2010, pp. 151–61. *DOI.org (Crossref)*, https://doi.org/10.1016/j.chb.2009.10.011.

9. "Re:Work – Learning & Development Guide: Create an Employee-to-Employee Learning Program." Rework.Withgoogle.Com (website) 4 Oct., 2022, https://rework.withgoogle.com/guides/learning-development-employee-to-employee/steps/introduction/.

10. Sim Sitkin. "Learning through Failure - the Strategy of Small Losses." *Research in Organizational Behavior*, vol. 14, Jan. 1992, pp. 231–66.

11. Zimmerman, Barry J. "Becoming a Self-Regulated Learner: An Overview." *Theory Into Practice*, vol. 41, no. 2, May 2002, pp. 64–70. *DOI.org (Crossref)*, https://doi.org/10.1207/s15430421tip4102_2.

12. Schunk, Dale H., et al. *Motivation in Education: Theory, Research, and Applications*. Pearson, 2014.

13. Chick, Nancy. "Metacognition." *Vanderbilt University,* 2013, https://cft.vanderbilt.edu/guides-sub-pages/metacognition/.

14. Raitner, Marcus. "On Top of Mount Stupid." *Medium,* 7 Oct. 2020, https://marcusraitner.medium.com/on-top-of-mount-stupid-9d38d1569225.

15. Frank, Thomas. "How to Learn Faster with the Feynman Technique (Example Included)." 7 Feb. 2017. YouTube video, 5:47. https://www.youtube.com/watch?v=_f-qkGJBPts.

16. Almarode, John. "Success Criteria: An Essential (and Often Underutilized) Component of Teacher Clarity." *Corwin Connect,* 3 Feb. 2021, https://corwin-connect.com/2021/02/success-criteria-an-essential-and-often-underutilized-component-of-teacher-clarity/.

SIX

MAKE AN INTELLECTUAL CONNECTION

We're about to walk down the intellectual path of learning, but first, we should define what we mean by the term *learning*. The American Psychological Association provides us with this definition:

> *Learning. noun.* the acquisition of novel information, behaviors, or abilities after practice, observation, or other experiences, as evidenced by change in behavior, knowledge, or brain function. Learning involves consciously or nonconsciously attending to relevant aspects of incoming information, mentally organizing the information into a coherent cognitive representation, and integrating it with relevant existing knowledge activated from long-term memory.[1]

Let's unpack this definition of learning, as there are lots of complex elements and terms jammed into those two sentences. First, learning means we take in some new information through observing others, reading a book, practicing, experiencing, and the like. We take in this information, we make meaning of it, we connect it to what we already know, and we store it in our memory. As a result of this process, we can change our behavior. We can do something we couldn't do before or do something in a new way.

In essence, learning in the workplace requires making useful memories—ones we can use to change our behaviors and improve our performance. One important thing to know is that learning is a use-it-or-lose-it proposition. We need to use the knowledge we have if we want to keep it. That's how practice and repeated exposure to information can help us keep learning fresh, but we all know what it's like to lose knowledge and skills because of a lack of application. In short, we forget.

This impermanence of memory highlights the importance of addressing our holy trinity, or fire triangle if you prefer: the emotional, intellectual, and strategic. We need an emotional connection to be willing to go through the practice and experiences necessary to acquire information and make these new memories. We need to make the intellectual connection to take in, process, and retain that information as memories. And we need to then have a strategic application for that learning. We need a way to use it, both to make the learning worth doing and to ensure it endures.

Our work in this chapter is to understand knowledge acquisition and application process: the sensing and sense-making, connection, and retention of learning. The UDL **Principle of Representation** helps leverage decades of research in cognition to anticipate and address likely barriers to intellectual connection, the "what" of learning, as David Rose calls it.[2]

Representation: The *What* of Learning

The mind is an amazing thing, gathering electrical impulses from various sensory organs in the body, combining and filtering them, and examining the ensuing amalgam to make sense of whatever is going on outside the body. However, your brain can't process all the stimuli it gets at once. It must prioritize. After processing the designated portion of available information, the brain then must decide what to do with it. So, how does your brain decide what's worth holding on to? What's important enough to be learned?

Since the 1950s, researchers have been developing and refining the information processing model (IPM) to describe the process of gathering, decoding, storing, and retrieving information.[3] This model, pictured in figure 6.1, consists of three components, or stores, of memory: sensory, working, and long-term. Think of them as stops on a journey. To move information between stops, there are three processes: selecting, organizing, and integrating.

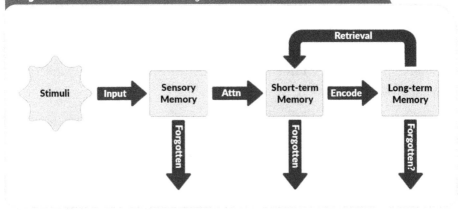

Figure 6.1 The Information Processing Model

The **Principle of Representation** takes what we know about each stage and provides guidance for supporting learning from start to finish, including how to make sure the learning endures over time.

Sensory Memory: The Journey Begins

Right now, your senses are taking in stimuli from the world around you: sights, sounds, smells, the works. That information is being sent to your **sensory memory store**, the first stop on the journey to memory.[4] The key to getting information into the senses and moving it on to the next step, working memory, comes down to two key elements: accessibility and attention.

Accessibility

Accessibility means the extent to which information exists in my space and in a format I can sense and use. As with so many things, accessibility is variable and subject to context. Let's take this book. If you're reading a physical copy of this book, it means the book physically exists in your space and in a format (ink or Braille print) that your senses can perceive. Let's say the book is in printed type and you're reading it—it's accessible. Now, if you turn off all the lights in your space, it's no longer accessible. However, if it's in Braille, it may still be accessible, but only if you were trained to read through touch.

We know from neuroscience that people perceive information differently. They may have a learning disability or an impairment to vision, hearing, or other sense. We also know that there is variability in the speed at which we can sense information. So, we must examine our environments for any barriers to access and attention with an awareness that others may experience the environment differently from ourselves.

Choices in media delivery (text, video, or audio) are increasingly showing up in customer environments, especially in the digital realm. Peruse various news outlets online and you'll find videos with a text transcription and articles that come with the option to read or listen. People are increasingly reading with their ears, preferring to consume information while driving, walking, or working on other tasks that require their vision.

Attention

Sensory memory can hold a lot of information but for only a very brief amount of time, and only a small amount can pass through to working memory. Stealing a term from the world of technology, **bandwidth** is the capacity for data transfer; for our purposes, we think of bandwidth as the maximum amount of data that can pass from sensory to working memory.[5] Bandwidth is finite, so our brains must prioritize. This is the process of **selection**;[6] conscious attention determines what makes it from sensory to working memory. If learners aren't engaged and attending to the information you want them to process, there's little chance of any learning taking place. Once we have their attention, we need to make sure the information is accessible and not presented at a pace that overwhelms the available bandwidth.

Learning Styles

When I discuss strengths or limitations based on format, I am not endorsing the concept of learning styles, in which people fall into one of three categories—visual, auditory, or kinesthetic learners—and should be supported in that primary modality, regardless of content or context. This theory, though widely propagated, has been thoroughly and repeatedly debunked.

Some things are best shared visually, maps for example. You might consider yourself an auditory learner, but unless you are visually impaired, a map is likely much more useful than is an auditory description of a landscape. Rather than this one-way-only approach, what about providing both the map *and* the audio that helps us make sense of that map?

In the last chapter, we talked about how to get an emotional connection going, which can fuel our commitment to paying attention. We can also support that by guiding attention, using cues to focus the learner's attention and eliminating distracting elements that might divert attention away from the learning. This is where our empathic approaches from chapter 3 can be so valuable. Experience the environment with your senses (i.e., go and see). What do you see, hear, smell, feel? How do others experience that same space, and what can that tell you about how to support greater accessibility of information? What about how they choose to access information? What helps or hinders attention?

Finally, we must think about how the conditions in the environment may shift; for example, are there times when the space is noisier, creating barriers to both hearing and attention? If so, what can we introduce into the environment to mitigate those barriers? Can we provide supports to mitigate the noise? As I've been writing this book, in my home that I share with my wife and children, I frequently use countermeasures such as noise-cancelling headphones and white noise to help me attend to the task at hand.

The more flexibility we can provide in the pace and format of information, the more available and accessible it will be to our various learners. Look for opportunities to provide the information in multiple formats. For example, providing captions to videos can support those who are hearing impaired, are in loud spaces, or are in quiet spaces without headphones and want to avoid disturbing others. Likewise, having audio versions of written materials can help those with visual impairments as well as those who need to access that information in a way that doesn't compromise their vision, such as people who are driving, walking, or otherwise on the move.

Here's an example from my own practice of providing alternatives for auditory and visual information. A few years ago, I was wrapping up a two-day workshop on Universal Design for Learning with several dozen new participants. Throughout the workshop, I required groups to collaboratively explore various resources I had supplied digitally—videos, articles, templates, and the like. Each video was captioned, and I also provided audio versions of each article, having recorded narrations of them on my laptop days before. I also provided paper versions whenever possible.

UDL CONNECTION

The first Guideline in the **Principle of Representation**, "Provide Options to Support Perception," focuses on getting information through the sensory memory store and into working memory. Here are the three checkpoints in that Guideline, followed by questions based on each. You can use these to pinpoint barriers in the learning environment.

"Provide Options to Support Perception"
- Offer ways for customizing the display of information.
    - To what extent can learners make decisions about how best to approach the learning and play to their strengths, interests, or preferences?
- Offer alternatives to auditory information.
    - To what extent are learners forced to rely on their hearing to receive information?
- Offer alternatives to visual information.
    - To what extent are learners forced to rely on their visual perception to receive information?

You can learn more about this Guideline and its checkpoints in appendix A.

As participants were filling out their feedback forms, one woman pulled me aside. She told me, "You know, this is the first training like this where I've been able to use everything."

"What do you mean?" I asked.

"I have a visual impairment. Being able to zoom in, to listen, and to use the accessibility tools in my browser to explore all the materials has been amazing."

I was a bit surprised. She had been an active participant, contributing to many conversations and making small talk with me during breaks, but never once did she ask about accessibility.

"I had no idea you had a visual impairment."

"Yeah, that's the point!" she said, "I didn't need to tell you because everything worked for me."

Working Memory

With our attention focused on accessible information, we are maximizing bandwidth into working memory, where our brains make sense of what we sense. Once again, variability is going to be the norm. We each process information in our own unique way, based on a combination of perception, experience, and genetics. If we aren't careful, we can put learners in environments that overwhelm or otherwise hinder their ability to make sense of information.

Working memory is a place for organizing information— sifting through to find patterns, draw connections, and make meaning of what we are taking in.[7] Think about the words you are reading right now. Your brain is getting visual information about variance in color and contrast that it recognizes as symbols (letters) and symbols arranged in patterns (words), and it's drawing a connection not only to what those individual words could represent but what the combination of those words means. All of that is happening in working memory.

People are, well, human, and so our ability to process information has its limits. To deal with those limits, we make decisions about where we will direct and sustain our mental focus. These limits are variable. Each person's limit is based on context, content, and innate capacity. When we operate within our limits, we're able to effectively deal with all that's piled on our mental plate. However, if we exceed our limits, we experience feeling overwhelmed. We can't take all the information coming at us, so we take steps to reduce the load. Feeling overwhelmed can be very stressful, and stress can often lead us to behaviors that, in calmer times, we'd choose to avoid. We might lash out, shut down, or just leave the situation all together.

We've all been there, especially during the COVID-19 pandemic. We're trying to focus on challenging work—a report, a design, a book—in our makeshift home offices. We try hard to blot out distracting noises, doing our best to stay on track. Then, someone or something else intrudes on our attention: a phone ringing, pop-ups taking over our screen, toddlers squabbling over toys. We growl in frustration, we yell for quiet, or we pound our desks in frustration.

Cognitive neuroscience has given us a wealth of insight into the limits of processing, the variability of those limits, and the ways that ineffective learning environments can rob us of vital processing capacity. The more environments make it hard for us to actually get to what we're supposed to learn and do, the more processing time and energy are required to meet our goals. Understanding the cognitive demands an environment can place on learners informs our expectations for their ability to access and process complex information.

It's not about just putting people in the proximity of information. They need support to make sense of what they're supposed to assimilate and connect it to what they already know and what they want to do. Processing information is, in a way, like solving a puzzle. If you've ever assembled a jigsaw puzzle, you know it's helpful, sometimes even essential, to have a picture of the completed product to reference when assembling the pieces. That picture is helping us orient the individual pieces to the whole; without it, we're going to have a really hard time unless the puzzle is extremely simple (and then, what's the point?).

> **Cognitive Load Theory**
>
> Much of this section is based on the cognitive load theory of working memory, pioneered by researchers such as John Sweller.
>
> The concepts of complexity, connection, and coherence closely align to what Sweller calls intrinsic, germane, and extraneous cognitive load. Rather than use that esoteric terminology, I've opted for simpler, more accessible language.
>
> If you'd like to learn more about cognitive load theory, the information processing model, and more, I highly recommend Richard Mayer's *Applying the Science of Learning*. See the resources section of this chapter for more information.

That picture is a countermeasure in the environment to support processing. Our charge as L&D partners is to anticipate barriers to processing and provide countermeasures that allow the bulk of a learner's limited capacity to be focused on the actual learning that needs to happen. We do this by lending clarity to the learning; facilitating connections to learners' purpose, experience, and prior knowledge; and reducing or eliminating any distractions or friction in the delivery. We do this through the three C's: clarity, connection, and chunking.

Clarity

Clarity is highly conducive to learning. The more easily I can determine what I'm looking at, being told, or reading, the more easily I can make connections to what I already know as well as what I'm trying to do. That puzzle picture provides clarity: This is what you're supposed to make out of those 500 pieces. Without that picture, without clarity, it becomes a much bigger lift.

Unfortunately, there are numerous barriers to clarity in everyday sharing of information, starting with the language we use to communicate our ideas. If we are receiving information in our primary language (for me, it's English), our working memory can make quick work of the sounds we hear or the symbols we see or touch. However, information in a nonprimary language (for me, non-English) requires us to devote some mental energy to translation. The less fluent we are in the language, the more mental energy we devote to translating the information, leaving us with less energy to process its deeper meaning.

Then there's jargon. Many of us love to use jargon, especially when it communicates our expertise. It also helps us to take conversational shortcuts. Why say "as soon as possible" when you can say "ASAP"? If everyone knows the jargon, we all can communicate. However, we can create barriers for people who are not up to date on all our specific terminology.

We can support clarity by examining the language, symbols, and other representations of information we use. For example, we are better able to retain information presented with words and visuals than with words alone, a phenomenon that researchers call the **picture superiority effect**.[8] Graphics can augment the meaning communicated through written or spoken language. After all, if a picture is worth a thousand words, that's a remarkably efficient way to communicate.

We can also provide support for those whose primary language is not the same as the information they're trying to process. In addition to added visuals, there are a host of translation tools available to help people translate information in real time. Further, providing some flexibility in the timing of that translation, such as sharing information in advance so people have time to process it at their own pace before coming together to build on it, allows everyone to start in the same place with their understanding of the content.

Finally, the way we organize information is important. The more logically we can arrange new pieces of information, the more readily people can make connections between the pieces as well as to their prior knowledge. Having reference points (e.g., the picture of the completed puzzle) and other organizing tools to point learners toward relevant information can reduce the friction in their ability to develop a clear understanding.

Connection

Speaking of understanding, variability is once again in play because knowledge and skill in a particular area will vary between people, and we need to account for that variability. Why? Well, for working memory to do its job, it relies on information in **long-term memory**—that's where your knowledge of letters, words, context clues, semantics, and the like resides. Working memory is making connections between the new information and existing information to make meaning, and if that meaning enhances the existing store of information, then that new information may get assimilated into long-term memory. This is the process of **integration**, the collaboration between working and long-term memory to make meaning and add to the long-term memory's store of information.

Once again, variability is the norm. Just as we can't assume everyone speaks the same jargon, or even the same primary language, we also can't assume that everyone has the same base level of knowledge in an area. With our diverse workforces, we can have a broad spectrum of knowledge and experience on the same team. Those who are experts in a particular area will more readily connect new learning to their significant storehouse of knowledge, while novices may not be able to independently connect new information to their emerging understanding.

Further, connection can often be difficult for those who haven't been asked or allowed to derive their own interpretation of new learning. If you've spent most of your life being told what to do and when to do it, you may not have fully developed the ability to think ahead, to wrestle with ambiguity, and to allow yourself the creative freedom to think up your own meaning for new information. Reinforcing the connection of the immediate content to the bigger picture allows people to create a bigger meaning for the learning, helping them orient new content to prior learning and even anticipate what's to come.

Chunking

Even with a focus on optimizing for complexity, we still must account for variability in each person's limit. According to cognitive neuroscience, our brains process a few chunks of information at a time; this represents our cognitive limit, the amount of information we can process at any one time.[9] A person's **cognitive limit** is based on two factors, one innate and the other contextual. Both factors are variable and relate to how our brains chunk information.

The first factor is the number of chunks a person can process at any one time. This is a product of biology and can vary from one person to another. This variability is best represented by a short range, though researchers debate the exact range (3 +/-1, 7 +/-2, and so on).[10] So, the 3 +/-1 range means that most people can handle 3 chunks, but for some it's 4, and for others, 2. As L&D folks, we're not going to know who's who, but we do have to anticipate that all won't process the same amount of information at the same speed.

Not only do we have varied numbers of chunks, but the size of those chunks differs based on a person's level of expertise in the content.[11] Experts can process far more in their chosen arena than novices can.[12] For example, an experienced software engineer would likely process code at a much faster rate than someone who is new to that discipline.

This is especially true of people who are learning content in a second or third language. Their chunk size may be limited not only by their knowledge of the content but by the language in which the content is being communicated. To be clear, they can still learn the content, but it will take longer, possibly significantly so, and they'll need a really strong emotional connection to persist. As L&D partners, we must be mindful that our learners will vary in their levels of expertise, so we need to be flexible in our pacing, facilitate connections to existing knowledge, and make sure that how we communicate supports understanding of what we're saying.

We can look at this limited capacity and appreciate the need for all three networks to work together. If I'm disengaged or under stress (emotions), my brain will prioritize vital chunks of my limited capacity (strategic) to thoughts and feelings other than what I'm supposed to be learning. A strong connection can reinforce processing by not only making ties to prior learning but also by reinforcing the emotional connection ("What's this got to do with me?") and making the learning the priority. We'll learn more about prioritization (i.e., executive functions) in the next chapter.

Clarity, connection, and chunking—that's what we can do for learners to support processing. We can take that further by being explicit in when, how, and why we are doing this, encouraging them to apply clarity, connection, and chunking into their own practices." Encouraging them to apply clarity, connection, and chunking into their own practices, in the emails they write, the presentations they develop, the instructions they give, and so on. In this way, they are facilitating their audience's learning and contributing to a culture of expert, collaborative learning.

The next Guideline in **Principle of Representation** is "Provide Options for Language and Symbols." Here we support clarity, connection, and chunking, using the five checkpoints below. Again, I've coupled each with a question that helps us interrogate our environments for barriers.

"Provide Options for Language and Symbols"
- Clarify vocabulary and symbols.
  - Might there be barriers because of jargon, esoteric language, or unfamiliar symbols?
- Clarify syntax and structure.
  - Is the message being conveyed simply and clearly?
- Support decoding of text, mathematical notation, and symbols.
  - Is the message structured to support accessible formats like Braille, text-to-speech, and so on?
- Promote understanding across languages.
  - To what extent are learners supported with access to information that is not in their first language?
- Illustrate through multiple media.
  - To what extent is written or spoken information paired with visuals (pictures, symbols, and so on) to enhance meaning?

You can learn more about this Guideline and its checkpoints in appendix A.

Long-Term Memory

A key characteristic of learning is that it endures over time. Brief retention is not learning; therefore, long-term memory is our target. We want our learners not only to process information but to retain it so they can use it later. Working memory and long-term memory work together through a process called **integration**, which connects what's currently being processed to prior learning.[13] That connection helps us do two things: assimilate new learning into our understanding and retrieve existing learning to understand current challenges.

Let's start with how we store new information for later use. There are two methods of integrating information into long-term memory: relation and rehearsal. **Relation** occurs when you learn a new tidbit about something with which you're familiar. **Rehearsal**, or what many people would call memorization, occurs when you don't have any prior learning with which to connect the new learning. If you repeatedly load the information into working memory, say, by saying or writing something over and over, your brain will eventually make space for it.[14]

Rehearsal is horribly inefficient compared to relation, but we can use some strategies to create artificial relationships to prior knowledge. For example, mnemonics are ways to tie unfamiliar information to common knowledge by word substitution, alliteration, music or rhyme, and so forth. The acronym ADDIE helps us remember the steps for that instructional design model: Analysis, Design, Development, Implementation, and Evaluation. It's a method of facilitating connection, our friend from the earlier section on working memory.

Teaching people to create their own mnemonics has been shown to greatly increase their capacity for retaining information for an extended period and changes the way their brains function when storing information.[15] This is big, because it means that a person's ability to store that information is variable and can be enhanced through training and deliberate practice. By creating their own memory-enhancing mnemonics, they're acting as expert learners, building their personal toolbox of strategies for remembering important information in ways that are personal and effective.

Relating new information to prior knowledge is a powerful mechanism for learning that we can leverage as L&D partners. The more we can support learners in connecting the new learning to what they already know, the better they'll be able to process, retain, and retrieve that information. However, there is, of course, a catch: Prior knowledge is variable. Some of our learners may not have learned as much about the content as others. Some may have learned the information but not have retained it. This is because long-term memory, though seemingly infinite in capacity, can be finite in duration. Real learning endures over time, so not only do we need to support variability in acquiring new knowledge, we have to anticipate barriers to retention.

As L&D partners, we may be well equipped to determine which pathway to retention—rehearsal or relation—is likely to be the most effective. However, if we want to build and support a culture of expert learning, we must help our learners understand these two pathways and the strategies they can use to make memory in each. By continuing to enhance their understanding of how they learn, we increase their ability to learn what they need, when they need to, where they are. Building capacity to make memory is key, but it's not enough. We also need to support the application, retention, and refinement of those memories.

Use It Or Lose It

You may be familiar with the **learning curve**, the rate of a person's progress in gaining new knowledge and skills,[16] but did you know that the learning curve has a sibling? It's called the forgetting curve, and the science behind it dates back more than 130 years. In 1885, Hermann Ebbinghaus published groundbreaking research on the psychology of memory. He found that memory of specific knowledge and skills (i.e., learning) degrades over time, and this degradation is correlated with the use of that knowledge. In short, if we don't use it, we lose it. Therefore, finding opportunities to apply knowledge and skills and to generalize their use to multiple contexts is crucial to maintaining and building upon learning.

What Do I Do With This?

A big element in retaining both an intellectual and emotional connection to learning is having a clear understanding of how the information might be used to do something. When we take information and apply it to a new context, also known as transfer, we strengthen that new learning in the process. If you follow even one of the recommendations in this book, you will be transferring the knowledge from this broad source and applying it to a specific context. That application will make the information you transferred more useful in general (having a stronger emotional connection) and memorable (having a stronger intellectual connection). Remember, learning is something that occurs through practice and experience and endures over time, so exposure to new information is largely wasted unless we allow learners the opportunity to apply it. And that opportunity has to come hard on the heels of that new learning, as the forgetting curve has repeatedly shown.

We can be effective partners by explicitly connecting new knowledge to the work and goals of learners and by providing opportunities to make that transfer, better cementing the learning in their memories. The more we can do this within the learning environment, the better. After all, the closer the learning is to the work, the faster it can be applied. If you can't get the learning any closer to the work, try to bridge the gap with some authentic practice to keep reinforcing and refining their new understanding. If it's formal learning (a training course or coaching session, for example) we can provide opportunities and support. We can ask learners to consider how they might use the new information, allowing for discussion and brainstorming.

UDL CONNECTION

The next Guideline in the **Principle of Representation** is "Provide Options for Comprehension." Here, we support clarity, connection, and chunking using the four checkpoints below. Again, I've coupled each with a question that helps us interrogate our environments for barriers.

"Provide Options for Comprehension."
- Activate or supply background knowledge.
  - To what extent are all learners supported in connecting new learning to their prior knowledge and skills?
- Highlight patterns, critical features, big ideas, and relationships. (8.2)
  - To what extent are all learners supported in connecting new learning to the big picture?
- Guide information processing and visualization
  - To what extent is the content chunked and sequenced to support processing and comprehension?
- Maximize transfer and generalization. (8.3)
  - To what extent are all learners supported in applying new learning to their work?

You can learn more about this Guideline and its checkpoints in appendix A.

We can simulate work applications and allow them opportunities for safe, deliberate practice. We can facilitate goal setting and planning for application upon their return to work, and we can highlight the benefits of improved performance, for them, for the team, for the organization, and for the customers. Within the work setting, we can build their capacity to support each other's practice by roleplaying applications, collaboratively brainstorming, providing feedback, and creating sandbox environments for safe application and experimentation. We can work with management to reinforce the application of learning and provide exemplars of practice that people can use as reference materials. Finally, we can serve as an on-call resource to support folks in the field.

Resourceful and Knowledgeable

Expert learners are resourceful and knowledgeable. They understand how they learn and have developed the ability to locate, select, and apply strategies to enhance their learning. They can also readily transfer that learning into authentic application. Every organization needs people who are resourceful and knowledgeable. Our work is to understand what it takes to build capacity for expert learning and then to meet our learners where they are and support their progress from novice to expert learner. We must also be mindful that barriers may still arise—barriers to access, to clarity, to connection, to transfer, and so on. Therefore, we must work with our learners to identify these barriers, develop countermeasures, and support the strategic application of these countermeasures by learners so they can continue to practice expert learning. And that's what it is: a practice, one that must be established, informed, reinforced, and refined to achieve maximum performance improvement.

Reflect and Connect

- We've learned that we need alternative paths into sensory memory so that having a single modality (audio, visual, or other) doesn't present a barrier to our various learners. How do you currently provide options for perception, and where are the opportunities to expand that practice?

- Clarity of language allows us to better process information. Where do you see jargon, esoteric terms, or convoluted language showing up in your workplace? What might you do to support your people to both deal with these existing barriers and learn to avoid creating those barriers for others?

- You've learned a lot already since you've started reading this book, including how the transfer of learning increases both retention and perception value. What plans have you set or might you set for applying your learning?

Resources

My favorite classes in graduate school were those that delved into the science of learning. I didn't want this book to be a collection of esoteric theories and research studies; however, if you want to go deeper into the cognitive neuroscience and psychology of learning and behavior, here are a few good starting points:

- **Khan Academy** has several videos you may find helpful, including topics such as cognitive load theory, the information processing model, and the spotlight model of attention. Just go to KhanAcademy.org and get access to these and other topics for free. Also, these videos are examples of some of the key concepts we have covered in this chapter. They provide information in both visual and audio formats, they are captioned, and there's a transcript available if you would prefer to just read the content.

- *How Learning Happens: Seminal Works in Educational Psychology and What They Mean in Practice* by **Paul A. Kirschner and Carl Hendrick**. The authors have selected more than two dozen important research articles and systematically broken each into more accessible, practical terms. Though framed more toward the realm of education, these studies cover valuable concepts for L&D, including prerequisites for learning, learning culture, and cautionary tales (looking at you, learning styles).

- *Applying the Science of Learning* by **Richard Mayer**. Mayer provides us with an excellent guide for putting research into action. This is one of the books I keep close at hand as I design to remind me of the *why* behind the various strategies and tactics I employ. You can learn more about this book at https://www.pearson.com/us/higher-education/program/Mayer-Applying-the-Science-of-Learning/PGM53979.html.

Resources

1. *Learning – APA Dictionary of Psychology*. https://dictionary.apa.org/learning. Accessed 26 Nov. 2021.

2. Meyer, Anne, et al. *Universal Design for Learning: Theory and Practice*. 1st ed., CAST Professional Publishing, 2014.

3. Schraw, Gregory, and Matthew McCrudden. "Information Processing Theory." *Education. Com*, 2009, https://project542.weebly.com/uploads/1/7/1/0/17108470/information_ processing_theory__education.com.pdf.

4. Schraw, Gregory, and Matthew McCrudden. "Information Processing Theory." *Education. Com*, 2009, https://project542.weebly.com/uploads/1/7/1/0/17108470/information_ processing_theory__education.com.pdf.; Atkinson, R., and R. Shiffrin. "Human Memory: A Proposed System and Its Control Processes." *The Psychology of Learning and Motivation: Advances in Research and Theory*, vol. 2, Academic Press, 1968.

5. Miller, Earl K., and Timothy J. Buschman. "Working Memory Capacity: Limits on the Bandwidth of Cognition." *Daedalus*, vol. 144, no. 1, Jan. 2015, pp. 112–22. *DOI.org (Crossref)*, https://doi.org/10.1162/DAED_a_00320.

6. Atkinson and Shiffrin; Schraw, Gregory, and Matthew McCrudden. "Information Processing Theory." *Education.Com*, 2009, https://project542.weebly.com/uploads/1/7/1/0/17108470/ information_processing_theory__education.com.pdf.

7. Atkinson, R., and R. Shiffrin. "Human Memory: A Proposed System and Its Control Processes." *The Psychology of Learning and Motivation: Advances in Research and Theory*, vol. 2, Academic Press, 1968.

8. Defeyter, Margaret Anne, et al. "The Picture Superiority Effect in Recognition Memory: A Developmental Study Using the Response Signal Procedure." *Cognitive Development*, vol. 24, no. 3, July 2009, pp. 265–73. *ScienceDirect*, https://doi.org/10.1016/j.cogdev.2009.05.002.

9. Atkinson, R., and R. Shiffrin. "Human Memory: A Proposed System and Its Control Processes." *The Psychology of Learning and Motivation: Advances in Research and Theory*, vol. 2, Academic Press, 1968.; Gobet, F., and G. Clarkson. "Chunks in Expert Memory: Evidence for the Magical Number Four… or Is It Two? Memory." *Memory*, vol. 12, no. 6, 2004, pp. 732–47, https://doi.org/DOI 10.1080/09658210344000530.; Miller, George. "The Magical Number Seven, plus or Minus Two: Some Limits on Our Capacity for Processing Information." *The Psychological Review*, vol. 63, no. 2, 1956, pp. 81–97.

10. Gobet, F., and G. Clarkson. "Chunks in Expert Memory: Evidence for the Magical Number Four… or Is It Two? Memory." *Memory*, vol. 12, no. 6, 2004, pp. 732–47, https://doi.org/DOI 10.1080/09658210344000530.; Miller, George. "The Magical Number Seven, plus or Minus Two: Some Limits on Our Capacity for Processing Information." *The Psychological Review*, vol. 63, no. 2, 1956, pp. 81–97.

11. Egan, D. E., and B. J. Schwartz. "Chunking in Recall of Symbolic Drawings." *Memory and Cognition*, vol. 7, 1979, pp. 149–58.

12. Groot, Adriaan David Cornets de. *Thought and Choice in Chess*. Mouton, 1965.

13. Schraw, Gregory, and Matthew McCrudden. "Information Processing Theory." *Education. Com*, 2009, https://project542.weebly.com/uploads/1/7/1/0/17108470/information_ processing_theory__education.com.pdf.; Mayer

14. Miller, George. "The Magical Number Seven, plus or Minus Two: Some Limits on Our Capacity for Processing Information." *The Psychological Review*, vol. 63, no. 2, 1956, pp. 81–97.; Mayer, Richard E. *Applying the Science of Learning*. Pearson/Allyn & Bacon, 2011.; Schraw, Gregory, and Matthew McCrudden. "Information Processing Theory." *Education. Com*, 2009, https://project542.weebly.com/uploads/1/7/1/0/17108470/information_

processing_theory__education.com.pdf.; Atkinson, R., and R. Shiffrin. "Human Memory: A Proposed System and Its Control Processes." *The Psychology of Learning and Motivation: Advances in Research and Theory*, vol. 2, Academic Press, 1968.

15. Dresler, Martin, et al. "Mnemonic Training Reshapes Brain Networks to Support Superior Memory." *Neuron*, vol. 93, no. 5, Mar. 2017, pp. 1227-1235.e6. *ScienceDirect*, https://doi.org/10.1016/j.neuron.2017.02.003.

16. "Learning Curve." *Lexico Dictionaries | English. www.lexico.com*, https://www.lexico.com/definition/learning_curve. Accessed 1 Aug. 2020.

SEVEN

MAKE A STRATEGIC CONNECTION

Let's remember the whole purpose of learning: to change behavior in order to improve performance so that individuals, teams, and organizations can innovate and thrive in this changing world of work. Passive learners wait for someone else to tell them what to do. Self-directed learners set goals but may lack the skill to pursue them effectively. Expert learners possess a bias for action—a mindset for proactively and strategically meeting, and often exceeding, expectations. We can partner with our people by building their skills to strategize and execute and creating the conditions that support them to act like expert learners.

As you likely deduced from the name, the UDL **Principle of Action and Expression** is about *doing*—creating, communicating, and planning. As we learned earlier, expert learners are strategic and goal-directed, and we as L&D partners have to know how to support them to act that way. We're going to look at the types of tools and spaces we provide to our people so that everyone can participate and contribute fully. We're also going to look at the contexts and processes we can create as L&D partners to support that doing. Finally, we're going to explore how to enhance and harness their ability to think strategically: to set goals, make plans, leverage supports, and adjust as needed to achieve or even surpass those goals.

The Baseline and Blue Sky of Access

Let's start by reengaging in the topic of accessibility. In chapter 6, we focused on the accessibility to receive information. Now, we need to think about the accessibility of output. Do we have the right tools and spaces that will allow everyone to share knowledge, ask questions, propose ideas, and so on? To inform that line of thinking, we can start with what's required under the law.

Title I of the Americans with Disabilities Act (ADA), the federal law protecting people with disabilities from discrimination, states that:

> [P]hysical and mental disabilities in no way diminish a person's right to fully participate in all aspects of society, but that people with physical or mental disabilities are frequently precluded from doing so because of prejudice, antiquated attitudes, or the failure to remove societal and institutional barriers.[1]

Notice how the legislators ascribed the barriers to the environment in which the person lives and works rather than to the person. Barriers exists in environments, not people. People with disabilities have a right to reasonable accommodations and assistive technology to ensure they are not unjustly prevented from participating in the workforce.

According to the ADA National Network, truly accessible technology can be used by people with a wide range of abilities and disabilities and incorporates principles of Universal Design so that each person can interact with the technology in ways that work best for him or her.[2] That means that a person with a disability can acquire the same information, engage in the same interactions, and enjoy the same services as a non.-disabled person in an equally effective, equally integrated manner, with substantially equivalent ease of use as a person without a disability.[3]

Here's the beauty of providing these tools and accommodations to all: Not only are we fulfilling our legal (and moral) obligations, but we may also be removing barriers for whom these supports were not specifically created. This is what's called the curb-cut effect, named for those shallow ramps installed at street corners across the globe. Curb-cuts are installed to fulfill the legal requirement to support people with impaired mobility who would struggle to traverse a sudden change in elevation. However, they're not the only ones who benefit from the existence of the curb-cut; cyclists, people pushing strollers or pulling hand carts, and many more all benefit from this simple ramp.

Universal Design "is the design and composition of an environment so that it can be accessed, understood, and used to the greatest extent possible by all people regardless of their age, size, ability, or disability" and, as you may have guessed from the name, a forerunner and inspiration for the creation of UDL.[4] It is a set of principles for designing physical spaces that have been influencing working and living spaces since the 1960s. Universal design seeks to eliminate physical barriers. UDL, in turn, expands the lens to encompass the intellectual and emotional space but does not leave the physical component behind because barriers to learning can be physical as well as intellectual and emotional.

The Fourth Dimension of Learning

When we consider the learning environment, and the potential barriers within it, we must consider not only the physical tools and spaces, but the ways that time can affect a person's ability to interact effectively in that environment.

Consider a conversation that moves faster than a hearing-impaired person can follow, let alone participate in. This is an example of temporal, or time-based, barrier.

When we anticipate such barriers, we can install some countermeasures, such as asynchronous discussion boards or practicing wait time while facilitating synchronous conversations.

What does this mean for our work? Well, first off, it can inform our assumptions about potential barriers. Just because our learners have not asked for accessibility tools or other supports, we can't assume no one needs them. The odds are that if we fail to address accessibility issues in our environments, we're likely to be putting barriers in for some learners. The pandemic has created a widespread awareness of the need for accessibility, particularly in our increasing use of technology to create and communicate.

Next, we can challenge ourselves to go beyond compliance and open our minds to what's possible if we intentionally address all barriers in the environment, not just those required by law, but those required for expert learning. This is the blue-sky mindset we must embrace if we are to be effective partners. Compliance is the baseline; supporting expert learning for all is the aspiration. Intentionally creating learning environments that account for variability in physical capacity lets those with physical challenges, temporary or permanent, feel as though they are welcome in that environment.

Once we have accessible spaces and tools, we need to address any barriers to using these tools and spaces to get things done. To survive and thrive in the rapidly changing world of work, we need to foster creativity, helping our people to develop new solutions to problems. We also want people to communicate effectively to better frame their challenges and opportunities and to share their learning with others, improving the efficiency and effectiveness of our teams and organizations.

UDL CONNECTION

The first Guideline in the **Principle of Action and Expression** is "Provide Options for Physical Action." We are establishing the baseline of access with an aspiration to continuously address barriers in pursuit of that blue-sky aspiration, learning environments that are truly born accessible.

"Provide Options for Physical Action"
- Vary the methods and pace for generation and communication. (3.1)
  - To what extent can everyone participate in conversations?
- Provide accessible tools, materials, and work environments. (3.2)
  - To what extent can every person navigate the workspace and interact with the physical tools without needing support?

You can learn more about this Guideline and its checkpoints in appendix A.

Creativity

Let's start by defining creativity. I went to Merriam-Webster, publisher of dictionaries for nearly two centuries, who essentially describe creativity as being able to bring something brand-new into existence. That's a start, but it's not particularly helpful. I can certainly make all kinds of things that have not yet existed, but to what end? The creation of an iceberg waxer would certainly be new, but not really of any use. That's where the late Sir Ken Robinson, author and educator whose TED Talk on how schools kill creativity has garnered 73 million views, comes to the rescue. He defined **creativity** as the process of having original ideas that have value.[5]

Notice how Robinson called it a process, not an innate ability. Other notable creative people agree. John Cleese, renowned comedic actor and humorist, says that creativity "is not a talent, it's a way of operating."[6] Creativity can be fostered and enhanced, but this requires intention. We can't just throw people in a room and tell them to be creative. After all, innovation is learning to do something new, or at least in a new way. So, creativity, like learning, is variable and contextual, and we in L&D can support creativity by creating the right conditions and building capacity.

Creativity requires us to do something new, so we need to understand how to create the space and processes to support that work. Numerous works provide deep dives into creativity, including some great ones that I've included in the resources section of this chapter. For our purposes, we're going stick to three core attributes: opportunity, safety, and flexibility.

Opportunity

The Minnesota Mining and Manufacturing Company, also known as 3M, is renowned as an innovative organization. Since its founding in 1902, 3M has evolved "from mining for rocks to rocking innovation," receiving more than 100,000 patents in the process.[7] A key driver of that innovative culture was William McKnight, an assistant bookkeeper who rose rapidly through the ranks and steered 3M for decades as president and, later, chairman of the board. McKnight's humble beginnings informed his perspective on the potential of his employees. His philosophy on fostering innovation was simple: Listen to anybody with an idea.

One of the biggest barriers to creativity is the assumption that creativity is a talent or innate ability and that we can spot that ability through outward manifestations such as hairstyle, attire, or even occupation. Many people believe that if you're creative, you don't wear a tie. They have established mental models of what creativity looks like, and our own mental models can be the biggest barriers to creativity. When we are so sure that our perceptions are reality, we can deny people, including ourselves, opportunities to be creative.

When it comes to offering opportunities to others, we often rely on the notion that people who show ability should be given opportunity. However, if I'm never given opportunity, how can I ever grow and show my ability? In order to counter our potential bias, we must override our proclivity to be selective and include everyone in the opportunity. As inclusion advocates Emma Van der Klift and

Norman Kunc write, "Opportunity is determined by social convention, not ability. That is, opportunity is not afforded to those who are most able, but to those our society deems worthy of that opportunity."[8] This passage highlights the problem of gatekeeping for opportunity. The solution is, quite simply, to open the gate to all. Listen to anyone with an idea.

Further, communicate the belief that everyone can be creative and that those ideas are needed. Find examples of other nontraditional innovators, such as Bettie Nesmith Graham, inventor of Liquid Paper, and share them with your people. When those great ideas come, amplify them and the stories behind them. If Sarah in shipping comes up with a novel way of preventing lost parcels, then make sure everyone hears that story. Make a concerted effort to create new mental models of what a creative person looks like. In short, all students should be able to point to a role model and think, "They look like me."

Safety

We explored safety in chapter 5, but it's worth repeating: the trinity is continuously active. We must be emotionally secure enough to venture a new idea and to have our ideas interrogated by our peers. We must also know that supporting the ideas of others does not diminish our individual value; when the team wins, we all win.

We also need the grace to incubate ideas and find their value. Rarely do great ideas spring forth fully formed from the minds of their creators; they require some experimentation and iteration, or as I prefer to call it, tinkering. Tinkering is making lots of little adjustments that honor and improve upon the original idea. Some ideas get tinkered with for years, but prolonged exploration of an idea has led to electric lights, airplanes, and, we hope, an eventual cure for cancer. Oh, and sticky notes.

Spencer Silver, a research scientist at 3M, spent years working on finding applications for an adhesive he'd created, one that stuck lightly to surfaces rather than bonding tightly.[9] He became known as Mr. Persistent because of his dogged pursuit, a pursuit made possible because the organization recognized the need to support experimentation instead of demanding immediate success. They knew he had an original idea; it just needed value.

That allowance of space paid off when a third aspect of creativity was engaged: community. There's a difference between having space and working in a silo; if we have ideas that can help the organization, we must allow others access to those ideas so that they can help with the tinkering. Silver didn't keep his light bonding adhesive to himself, he presented it to others at 3M. That openness allowed another 3M scientist, Art Fry, to match the idea with its value.

On Wednesday evenings, Fry would practice in his church choir, and he was frustrated because the little scraps of paper he used to mark the pages of selections within his hymnal were always falling out. He needed bookmarks that would stick but wouldn't damage the pages when they were removed. He needed Silver's adhesive. Silver and Fry partnered on the idea of using small bits of paper that were sticky on one side, and in the process, they created not only a more effective hymnal bookmark, but a whole new way of communicating.

A creative community is one that is willing and able to have constructive dialogue about ideas, offer and receive feedback, and share new discoveries. Knowledge is shared to the betterment of the organization. Such open communication requires systems of support (more on that coming up), but more important, it requires safety and belongingness. People need to be able to bring their whole selves to work. If Art Fry hadn't been comfortable talking about his religion and love of singing, he wouldn't have been able to tie value to Spencer Silver's idea.

Flexibility

A foundational element of Universal Design for Learning is the concept of firm goals, flexible means. We start with a clear, compelling purpose, but we remain open to a variety of possibilities in how we might meet those goals. This flexibility shows up in how we go about generating ideas and how we as L&D partners support ideation, experimentation, and implementation.

We need original ideas, and then we need to vet those ideas for viable application. These steps represent divergent and convergent thinking, a two-phase model for driving innovation. Using our definition of creativity, we can say that divergent thinking generates the original ideas, and convergent thinking looks for the ideas that have true value.

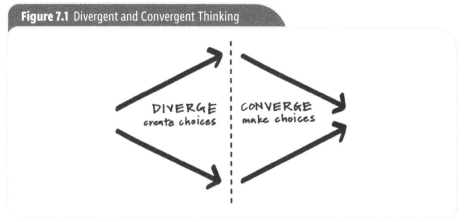

Figure 7.1 Divergent and Convergent Thinking

DIVERGE
create choices

CONVERGE
make choices

Credit: © 2023. IDEO, Inc. Used with permission.

Divergent thinking asks us to generate as many ideas as possible without imposing boundaries or imposed organization. To excel at this, you either need to disregard most of your mental models or you need to not have many in the first place (which is why young children are genius-level divergent thinkers[10]). In divergent thinking, there can be no wrong answers. This is essential; if we're afraid to be wrong, we can't be creative. Coaches and managers must allow for divergent thinking to occur if they truly want to foster creativity. Remember, we want original ideas.

Convergent thinking is a linear process of analyzing problems and finding viable solutions—solutions that have value. Convergent thinking is a necessary step for innovation; it's just not Step 1. If you start with convergent thinking, all those mental models, those ideas of what works and how things are done, will prevent you from considering novel approaches. So, to find new solutions, we need ideas that are born free of the mental frameworks under which we operate. That's why we must start with divergent thinking to generate original ideas and then hone those ideas to find actionable, impactful solutions—solutions that have value.

This creative process has been put simply as creating choices (divergent thinking) and then making choices (convergent thinking).[11] Fostering creativity is a hallmark of Universal Design for Learning—improving as designers, as learners, and as people is a journey, and one without a singular path to follow. We can't resort to the default; we continuously look for flexible, alternative paths.

There's no one right way to begin working creatively. We in L&D can support capacity-building by explicitly teaching a design process, helping learners build structures for divergent and convergent thinking. There are many models of design thinking, some more detailed than others, so provide a few options that people can experiment with and provide them in their contexts to see what works best.

We can also create space for creativity by providing optional activities (hack-a-thons, design labs, and so forth) that both facilitate the creative process and, potentially, serve as innovation engines, persuading leadership to make innovation time a fixture in people schedules. Google has their 20 percent time, a program that allows Googlers (Google-speak for employees) to spend 20 percent of their time on projects they think will help the company (i.e., generate original ideas that have value). They don't relegate that 20 percent time to one sector, say engineering or product design; everybody gets it.

To be fair, innovative as they are, the leaders at Google didn't invent 20 percent time, they just gave a 5 percent bump to an existing practice of 15 percent time that had been used for decades at 3M. 3M's leadership understood that people need not only the opportunity to pitch their ideas, but also the time and space to develop those ideas without overworking themselves or being chastised for working on non-sanctioned tasks. If they have to innovate on their own time and dime, they may assume their ideas are not valued and keep their innovations to themselves.

Communication

Organizations benefit when information moves efficiently. When individuals and teams share ideas, observations, challenges, and questions, it expands the opportunity to leverage different perspectives, experiences, and talents to capitalize on opportunities to innovate.

When information is not shared effectively, the performance levels of individuals, teams, and the organization suffer. Panopto, a tech off-shoot of Carnegie Mellon University, studied more than 1,000 workers, asking them how often they had to go looking for knowledge, how long they had to wait for answers, and other questions related to knowledge sharing.[12] On average, their participants reported spending:

- 5 hours per week waiting on others for knowledge

- 8 hours per week working inefficiently rather than wait for others to provide them with needed knowledge

- 6 hours per week duplicating the efforts of others

Like so many things related to learning and performance, our ability and motivation to communicate is variable, so it's imperative that we build capacity for effective communication and address any environmental barriers. For our purposes, we're going to divide our efforts to support communication into two areas: building capacity to use a variety of tools and media to communicate (the *how*) and fostering a culture of collaboration (the *why*).

The *How* of Communication

My dad is an engineer, and the best problem-solver I know. He has dozens of patents and has helped developed invaluable innovations, such as the first portable CT-scanner for mobile hospitals, blood cancer detectors, and nonlethal anti-vehicle defense systems. He's also dyslexic, which I didn't know until I joined the navy and would receive handwritten letters, complete with interesting spellings like "verry." If you asked him to write you detailed reports, it would take him a long time to communicate effectively.

When I was a kid, I asked him what he did for work every day. He told me.

> "I sit in meetings where a bunch of people talk about machines they want to make, and I sit there with my sketch pad and listen. When they're done talking, I hold up the drawing on my pad and say, 'You mean this?' and then they say 'Yes,' and then I'd go build it."

Imagine if his employers had required that all of his ideas be formulated in a typewritten narrative (looking at you, Amazon). There are many ways to share ideas. Right now, you may be reading printed text, or digital text, or even listening to these words. The important thing to remember is that we must value the message more than the medium in which the message is shared. Mandating a single method of sharing information creates potential barriers, stifling ideas and impeding innovation.

Within media, we should still consider options for how we create. Ponder this question: What is writing? Think about that for a minute—maybe jot down or just verbalize an answer. Now, does your definition include the tool used? For example, did it say "The act of committing thoughts to paper using a pen or pencil," or something to that effect? If so, think about this question: Is the tool the important thing, or is it the thinking?

Merriam-Webster[13] defines writing as:

1. the act or process of one who writes: such as the act or art of forming visible letters or characters, specifically: HANDWRITING

2. the act or practice of literary or musical composition

Definition 1 focuses on the physical act—it emphasizes handwriting, making a distinction between that act and other methods of "forming visible letters or characters" such as typing or dictating. Definition 2 focuses on the production of a composition—an intellectual creation. It says nothing of the method by which that composition is physically projected. This is the distinction inherent in providing options for physical action. Don't let the physical tool restrict the expression of the thinking because it's the intellectual creation that's most important.

When we restrict people to one tool for expression, we can unintentionally present them barriers whether through a gross or fine motor challenge, a lack of typing experience, or some neurological challenge like dyslexia. Can you tell by reading this whether I typed it, dictated it to a typist, or used speech-to-text? Can you tell how long it took to produce? The answer to both questions is "No" and, more to the point, why would you care? You care about the quality and relevance of what's written.

Of course, there are times when the tool *is* the point (i.e., a specific software application), and there's no substitute. In that case, you may consider the variability of your people to use that tool and provide options and supports for those who are less adept than others so that they can increase their skill. Just make sure you're always thinking about the goal and developing countermeasures to barriers in the environment so all can meet that goal.

Finally, consider building learners' capacity to communicate by developing their understanding of the trinity and barriers to learning. After all, they are trying to effectively share information, so understanding the variability in their audience where potential barriers might present themselves can help them to proactively design effective messages. Teach them the need to communicate value and connect the information shared to a goal or purpose. Help them make their messages clear, coherent, and connected to the big picture. Provide examples and non-examples of good communication and highlight what about each makes them more or less effective. Remember, we are building learners' capacity to be strategic and goal-directed, so they need the ability to make decisions based on how they want to approach the goal.

The *Why* of Communication

Along with the capacity to effectively communicate, we must make clear why communication is important and for the benefit of the individual, the team, and the organization. As we discussed in chapter 5, we have to incentivize knowledge sharing over knowledge hoarding. Highlight contributions to the team and the value of input, be it ideas, questions, or concerns.

We also must make that communication safe. Speaking up in meetings with colleagues and superiors can be intimidating, especially if the speaker anticipates the input might not be well received. Having alternate communication channels allows for expression without fear of reprisal. For example, during Lee Cockerel's tenure as executive vice president of operations at Walt Disney World, he had a dedicated voicemail and email for cast members (Disney's term for employees) to voice their input anonymously. Today, having this psychologically safe communication lane is common practice for Disney leaders.[14]

Create models and norms for communication, demonstrating what effective communication looks like and how to achieve it. Provide templates to support those who are still building their capacity for communication, highlight examples of effective communication, and model different forms of sharing knowledge so people know there's no one right way to communicate.

Strategic and Goal-Directed

The most successful organizations are those filled with people who can work independently and collaboratively to get things done without needing constant, specific direction. In the parlance of expert learning, we call this being strategic and goal-directed. Expert learners set their sights on meeting challenging goals, set plans to meet those goals, monitor their progress and adjust as necessary, and keep their focus on the work at hand. They have a bias for action and the tools to put that bias to good use.

Consider air traffic controllers. Every day in the United States, roughly 2.7 million people travel by air.[15] Air traffic controllers guide pilots and crews to taxi, take off, fly, and land safely. That's the goal of every day: tracking thousands of aircraft, monitoring weather and other conditions that can affect travel, adjusting flight plans as necessary, all to meet that goal of ensuing everyone is safe. Clearly, these men and women have to be strategic and goal-directed.

Our brains have their own version of the air traffic controllers that help us to set goals, make plans, track progress, and navigate changes. **Executive functions** are a set of cognitive tools our brains use to control our behavior, especially as we set and pursue goals.[16] The processes reside primarily in the brain's prefrontal cortex, often referred to as the air traffic control center of the brain. The prefrontal cortex monitors and directs other areas of the brain, keeping track of the goal and adjusting behavior to meet that goal in the context of current conditions and anticipated changes.[17]

Executive functions require three interrelated skills:

- working memory – our ability to hold and process information
- mental flexibility – our ability to focus and adjust our thinking based on current conditions and the goal
- self-control – our ability to set and pursue goals without being overly distracted

Executive functions are essential for our learners to make the behavioral changes we're trying to promote; however, not everyone comes to us with these traits, and not all work environments support people to act in this way. Executive functions are variable, contextual, and plastic. Let's explore a few reasons why.

First, there's human development. The prefrontal cortex becomes fully functional at different ages, usually by age 25. So, depending on the age of your learners, they may need more support to set and achieve goals. Further, people who are neurodiverse—they may have autism, attention-deficit/hyperactivity disorder (ADHD), or another of many neurological traits and may need different conditions to support their focus.

Along with neurological development, experience is another variable. Some people are coached to focus and think strategically, learning strategies and developing their own mental toolbox for getting things done, while others lag in their development of these key skills. Executive functions are plastic and improve with deliberate practice and authentic application.

Finally, the context of the learning can support or impede the learner's ability to focus. For example, do you ever seek privacy when you're trying to figure out how to do something for the first time? Whenever I am trying to fix something around my house, type, or do anything where I might make observable mistakes, I lose part of my working memory (remember our chunks from chapter 6) because I'm thinking about how my wife, colleagues, or children might react to my working my way through something hard. That's an emotional distraction, a barrier in the environment, and just one of many that can present themselves.

As L&D partners, we need to anticipate these areas of variability and environmental factors so that we can account for them effectively in our environments. We must anticipate varied levels of existing capacity, develop supports to buttress existing skills, and mitigate distractions and other barriers to strategic thinking and doing. We can explicitly teach how to focus, set goals, create plans, and shift plans based on changing conditions but only if we prioritize the development of these skills. Let's take a closer look at these "get stuff done" processes and see how we can be valuable partners to our people by addressing barriers and building capacity.

Goal Setting

Goal setting is adding some specificity to developing expectations for our learners—what exactly we are trying to do, by when, and what it would look like to meet the goal? There's a whole host of research on goal setting, going back decades. However, rather than delve into the esoteric, we're going to translate that valuable insight into action. If you want to dig deeper into that research, I've provided links to some further goal setting resources at the end of this chapter.

We can support goal setting by providing a clear structure to the process. There are many goal setting models you can use; I'm going to take one and apply the UDL lens to enhance the process by anticipating barriers and developing countermeasures. You may be familiar with the widely used strategy of setting SMART goals—ones that are **s**trategic, **m**easurable, **a**ttainable, **r**elevant, and **t**ime-bound. I first encountered them nearly two decades ago, but recently, I've encountered a newer approach—FAST goals. FAST goals require four elements:

- **Frequent**: Goals should be embedded in continuous discussions to inform self-assessment and strategic thinking and to provide feedback.

- **Ambitious**: The goal should be difficult, but not impossible.

- **Specific**: Goals have clear metrics that allow for specific success criteria and measurable progress.

- **Transparent**: Goals and current performance should be made public.

Let's compare FAST to SMART. Both include the need for specificity and measurement. However, FAST highlights the need for ongoing engagement with the goals and using progress and feedback so learners can see how they are progressing as well as how their actions are positively or negatively affecting their performance. As we learned in chapter 5, feedback enhances learner agency—they are doing the learning, it's not being done to them—and allows them to adjust as needed to meet or exceed the goal. FAST also focuses on goals that are ambitious rather than merely attainable. This adds the challenge needed to demonstrate that this goal builds learners' capacity and increases their sense of capability when they're able to meet this high expectation.

The creators of the FAST goal method, Donald and Charles Sull, assert that transparency provides the necessary accountability to achieve business goals. However, in a learning context, that transparency may be a barrier, depending on the level of psychological safety present in the team. To mitigate that threat, here are a few adjustments you can make:

- Make group FAST goals so learners share ownership of the goals.

- Limit the transparency to those providing and receiving feedback, minimizing the threat of peer judgment.

In my work, I've begun by co-constructing goals with my people; later, as the team has familiarity with the model, I revert to a more consultative role, allowing the team to have strong agency in their improvement. A key element of the goal setting is to develop examples of what it might look like to achieve the goal without mandating that it's the only way for that to happen. Unless the goal is to implement a process, don't make the process the goal. It's the outcome that is the goal, and that outcome may look different based on variability.

This is especially important when it comes to the "soft skills" such as collaboration and problem-solving. These traits are valuable, observable, and can produce great outcomes, but they shouldn't be measured by a standardized collaboration test or set of premade problems. Consider how learners might identify opportunities to develop these skills and develop authentic success criteria. Allow them to incorporate a variety of data sources, such as observations, interviews, and products, that allude to the skill being applied effectively. After all, the benefit to the individual is not being able to pass a contrived test but to improve their actual workplace performance.

Strategic Planning

Building on their setting of goals, individuals and teams will be even more empowered when they decide what it will look like to meet the goal and how they are going to make that happen. This is where the UDL philosophy of "firm goals, flexible means" becomes key—the flexibility of the pursuit as well as the success criteria we just discussed. Learners need to plan their own way to meet the goal; we in L&D can be supportive by ensuring there's an established planning process in place. Having a set process provides the necessary structure for our people to be intentional in their pursuit of improvement. It also facilitates collaborative planning and peer feedback as people develop a common methodology of planning.

You might be thinking, wait a second, why are we prescribing a process for planning if there's no one right way? If so, that's an excellent question. What we are doing is building capacity; once learners are familiar with a process and use it to plan individually and collaboratively to meet goals, teams can consider whether that model is best suited for their work or whether they might experiment with another. They can be expert learners in their iteration of the planning process, even offering options for teams, but first we must make sure everyone has the capacity to employ a structured planning process.

Locating and Leveraging Resources

To effectively create, execute, and adjust strategic plans, people need to know what they can use to get the job done. As we learned in our exploration of the modern learner, people are looking for resources they can access on the job so they can solve their problems in real time. L&D can support this by building capacity for effective knowledge management and providing flexible pathways for accessing necessary resources.

Managing Knowledge

As we learned earlier in this chapter, barriers to locating knowledge can lead to redundancy and inefficiency. All that time we spend searching for or recreating the knowledge we need to solve problems can't be replaced. In his book *Building the Learning Organization*, Michael Marquardt, professor of Human Resource Development and International Affairs at George Washington University, emphasizes the strategic importance of knowledge management: "Acquiring the ability to manage knowledge should become the primary job of every worker in every organization."[18]

Knowledge management solutions are, like most of what we've discussed in this book, contextual. There's no one right way to manage knowledge. Interactive databases such as Zendesk can support your team to organize, locate, retrieve, and build additional knowledge resources. Social tools such as Yammer, Slack, and others can help facilitate conversations between individuals and teams, increasing the breadth and speed of social learning. No matter what tools or systems your organization employs, we in L&D can apply our UDL lens to that work. If the goal is efficient, effective storage and retrieval of knowledge, we should examine the environment for barriers to that goal and deploy countermeasures to address them.

For example, let's say we're using a database system that uses a taxonomy, a system of tags for classifying and organizing items. We can anticipate that people will vary in their capacity to effectively use that database, so we should develop and distribute supports like quick reference guides and worked examples of categorization. These countermeasures can provide the necessary at-will support so that everyone can effectively utilize the tool.

Our people not only need access to the necessary learning, but they should also have the flexibility to choose the method of learning that best suits them. After all, we know there is no one right way to learn, so having options allows people to choose the method that best fits their strengths and preferences as well as the constraints of their context. Not everyone twill have the necessary room in their schedule for an extensive, synchronous online course, while others will prefer that structured, interactive experience.

L&D should, whenever possible, create a buffet of options in different media, depths, and lengths and build learner capacity to strategically select the resources that best support their plans for achieving goals. A great example of this approach is the Owens-Kadakia Learning Cluster Design model (OK-LCD). To learn more, check the resources section of this chapter.[19] Providing that flexibility both honors the autonomy of the learner and provides the flexibility to address learner variability.

Monitoring Progress

We've created goals, plans to meet them, and resources to support the plan, but how do we know whether our plans are working? Remember our air traffic controllers. They are continuously monitoring progress and conditions so they can make needed adjustments. Our people can't wait until the plan is fully executed to find out whether it's working; they need data and reference points so they can continuously gauge progress.

You wouldn't drive from Los Angeles to San Francisco by simply heading north for six hours and then seeing whether you can spot the Golden Gate Bridge; you'd use a GPS device or map app. If those weren't available, you'd stop to get directions or purchase a map. However, people may start with plans and then doggedly stick with those plans, ignorant of or ignoring information that signals a need for a course correction. Remember that one component of executive functions is mental flexibility—the ability to shift your thinking. This flexibility is variable, but it's also plastic.

We can support progress monitoring and plan adjustment by ensuring that people have the necessary data and reference points to accurately assess performance. Having clear success criteria is a start. If we have a solid picture of the end goal, we can backwards map some waypoints. If there are exemplars, previously created artifacts that meet the goal criteria, those can also serve as reference points. Having quality feedback loops can provide that GPS-style, real-time data to reinforce efforts and inform adjustments.

The best thing we can do for learners is help them to be proactive in their progress monitoring. They can't wait for the data to come to them; they must continuously inform their perspective by seeking out feedback, gathering data, and challenging their own assumptions. These efforts will keep them mentally flexible and build their agency in driving their own performance improvement. They won't need anyone from L&D to tell them whether they met their goals; they'll know it for themselves.

UDL CONNECTION

The final Guideline in the **Principle of Action and Expression** is "Provide Options for Executive Functions." We are supporting people to set goals, create plans to meet them, leverage resources in those pursuits, monitor progress, and adjust as needed.

"Provide Options for Executive Functions"
- Guide appropriate goal setting.
  - To what extent are learners capable and supported to create clear, challenging, measurable goals?
- Support planning and strategy development.
  - To what extent are learners supported to think strategically and plan effectively?
- Facilitate managing information and resources.
  - To what extent can every person identify, access, and leverage the knowledge and support necessary to meet the goal?
- Enhance capacity for monitoring progress.
  - To what extent can learners determine whether they're progressing toward their goal and when or whether plans must be adjusted?

You can learn more about this Guideline and its checkpoints in appendix A.

Expert learners are empowered and driven to continuously improve, innovate, and get hard things done. They select the tools and resources they need to be creative, share information, and solve novel problems. L&D can be supportive of expert learning by providing accessible tools and spaces; fostering and sustaining creative, collaborative cultures; and equipping people with the structures, skills, and resources to intentionally set and achieve goals.

Over the past three chapters, we've covered the pathways to expert learning and how we can be partners in supporting people along that journey. However, we can't do it alone. We need another set of partners—the leaders and managers—to foster and sustain a culture of expert learning.

Reflect and Connect

- Compliance is the baseline of accessibility, and it's foundational to creating flexible learning environments. Think about the tools you use in your daily work (computers, peripherals, and so on). How accessible are they, and how familiar are you with their accessibility supports? How might better understanding these options and supports improve your design efforts?

- Is there a dominant means of communicating ideas in your workplace (emails, slide shows, and so forth)? Where do you see opportunities to open up those communication lanes to more methods of expression?

- We know that learning is indirectly assessed and that learners need to "do" something to demonstrate learning. Often, what is done is based more on what is easier to measure (multiple choice, true false) than what best suits the learner, for example, performance, portfolio of evidence, or other. How do you tend to assess performance, and is there room to expand that practice to include ways that may be more meaningful, authentic, or representative of the learning?

Resources

- IDEO is a world-renowned leader in fostering design-thinking and innovation. Their online university, IDEOU.COM, provides courses, certifications, and resources for design-thinking, creativity, collaboration, and more.

- The Owens-Kadakia Learning Cluster Design (OK-LCD) model is a great approach for shaping behavior change by surrounding your learners with a variety of resources and then empowering them to strategically select, engage with, and leverage the resources. You can learn more at https://learningclusterdesign.com/, where you'll find videos, blog posts, and more. You'll also find information in their excellent book, *Designing for Modern Learning: Beyond ADDIE and SAM.*

- *Creativity: A Short, Cheerful Guide* by John Cleese. This is indeed short and cheerful in many formats. I prefer the audiobook because it's narrated by the author and takes just under an hour to enjoy.

Resources

1. ADA. "Americans with Disabilities Act of 2008." U.S.C., 110–325, 25 Sept. 2008.

2. *Glossary of ADA Terms | ADA National Network.* https://adata.org/glossary-terms. Accessed 9 Dec. 2021.

3. "What Is Accessibility?" *AEM Center,* https://aem.cast.org/get-started/defining-accessibility. Accessed 9 Dec. 2021.

4. CEUD. "What Is Universal Design?" *Centre for Excellence in Universal Design,* http://universaldesign.ie/What-is-Universal-Design/. Accessed 30 Mar. 2020.

5. Robinson, Ken, and Lou Aronica. *Creative Schools.* Penguin, 2016. p.118

6. Cleese, J. (1991). *Lecture on Creativity.* Retrieved from https://www.youtube.com/watch?v=Pb5oIIPO62g; Cleese, John. *Creativity: A Short, Cheerful Guide.* Crown, 2020.

7. *Timeline of 3M History | 3M United States.* https://www.3m.com/3M/en_US/company-us/about-3m/history/timeline/. US. Accessed 3 Oct. 2020.

8. Van Der Klift, Emma, and Norman Kunc. "Ability and Opportunity in the Rearview Mirror." *Working with Families for Inclusive Education: Navigating Identity, Opportunity and Belonging,* vol. 10, Emerald Publishing, Limited, 2017.

9. "History Timeline: Post-It Notes." *Post-It®,* https://www.post-it.com/3M/en_US/post-it/contact-us/about-us/. US. Accessed 3 Oct. 2020.

10. Land, George, and Beth Jarman. *Breakpoint and beyond mastering the future today.* HarperBusiness, 1992.

11. "IDEO Design Thinking." *IDEO | Design Thinking. designthinking.ideo.c*om, https://designthinking.ideo.com/. Accessed 4 Aug. 2020.

12. Panopto. "3 Ways Inefficient Knowledge Sharing Hurts Productivity At Work." *Panopto Video Platform,* 16 Oct. 2019, https://www.panopto.com/blog/how-much-time-is-lost-to-knowledge-sharing-inefficiencies-at-work/.

13. "Writing." Merriam-Webster Online, https://www.merriam-webster.com/dictionary/writing. Accessed 4 Sept. 2019.

14. Cockerell, Lee. *Creating Magic: 10 Common Sense Leadership Strategies from a Life at Disney.* Vermilion, 2009.

15. Federal Aviation Administration. *Air Traffic By The Numbers*. 27 May 2022, https://www.faa.gov/air_traffic/by_the_numbers/.

16. "Definition of Executive Function | Dictionary.Com." *Www.Dictionary.Com*, https://www.dictionary.com/browse/executive-function. Accessed 31 May 2021.

17. Funahashi, Shintaro, and Jorge Mario Andreau. "Prefrontal Cortex and Neural Mechanisms of Executive Function." *Journal of Physiology-Paris*, vol. 107, no. 6, Dec. 2013, pp. 471–82. *ScienceDirect*, https://doi.org/10.1016/j.jphysparis.2013.05.001.

18. Marquardt, Michael J. *Building the Learning Organization: Mastering the 5 Elements for Corporate Learning*. Davies-Black, 2002.

19. Kadakia, Crystal, and Owens, Lisa M.D. Designing for Modern Learning: Beyond ADDIE and SAM. ATD Press, 2020; LISA OWENS; CRYSTAL KADAKIA. DESIGNING FOR MODERN LEARNING. ASSOCIATION FOR TALENT DE, 2020.

EIGHT

PUT YOUR LEARNING TO WORK

We've been on quite a journey so far. We've spent the last several chapters learning what's needed for emotional, intellectual, and strategic connections to learning. And, though I've provided a few strategies and exercises along the way, much of this book has been directed at fostering your emotional and intellectual connections to the concept of expert learning. Now, we prepare for the next phase of your journey. To do that, I'm going to share some parts of my journey in hopes that you might draw some inspiration, but take this as advice, not a series of mandates. As always, there's no one right way to move ahead.

Years ago, I was faced with a tough assignment: leading a new team in a high-stress environment with very little in the way of organizational support. In my run-down office, directly across from my desk, I made a makeshift poster with this saying I took from Teddy Roosevelt (who, I later learned, had taken it from Billy Widener): "Do what you can, with what you've got, where you are."[1]

Balance your enthusiasm and expectations with a realistic assessment of your current capacity and sphere of influence. Take ownership of the learning environment, but realize that you may be limited, at least initially, in what you can directly control. Traditionally, L&D can have a lot of control over formal learning environments, and, to some extent, social learning as well. We set goals and expectations, we share resources, we create processes and activities to facilitate exploration and collaboration, and so on. However, we tend to have much less control over the working environment, where so much learning happens and needs to happen. By ourselves, we will struggle to mitigate certain barriers, such as misaligned incentive structures or convoluted communication systems. Over time, we can influence the culture (more on that later), but first, let's look at what we L&D folks already do and start slowly and smoothly to intentionally apply what we've learned together.

Begin Your Deliberate Practice

Supporting expert learning with UDL is something that takes a relatively short time to begin doing and a lifetime to master. The key is to commit to continuous deliberate practice. Start small, but don't stop there. In chapter 4, we explored Tom Tobin's Plus-One approach. (Please find a quick review on the next page.) Use this today, tomorrow, and every day you prepare for supporting learning. Build your proficiency anticipating and addressing barriers, and keep track of your successes, failures, and the lessons learned from each.

As you get used to thinking in this new way, look for opportunities to instill your learning into new learning environments you create or support, including workshops, e-learning modules, and presentations. The next few sections will help you begin designing goal-directed, flexible learning environments that embrace variability and support expert learning.

Start with Firm Goals

If you're an instructional designer, or you support others' designs, incorporate your new UDL lens into your existing design process. For instance, no matter what design methodology you use, you're to start with developing some clear, challenging goals. Along with firm goals, we need flexible means; make sure each goal allows for flexibility in how people achieve and demonstrate achievement of the goal. For example, if the goal is to describe a concept, allow for different ways of description (oral, written, visual, and so on).

Further, consider the trinity in your goal setting process. For the past few years, I have been going beyond setting intellectual goals and creating additional goals for emotional commitment and strategic application. I want my learners motivated to use what they know and have a plan for that application. For example, during a conference presentation, my co-facilitator and I set the following goals for our participants:

- Develop an initial emotional commitment to UDL implementation (affective)
- Describe the *why*, *what*, and *how* of UDL (recognition)

- Set a clear, measurable, time-bound goal for continuing your learning after this conference.
  - Optional: Select a partner, share goals, and plan for a follow-up conversation.

As we learned in chapter 4, our best designs are informed through empathy, so with your goals established, start thinking about how your learners are as people. Use your new UDL lens to enhance that work. What variability might exist in your audience that could affect the ways in which they connect emotionally, intellectually, and strategically to the learning? Reflect on past experiences. Where have your people struggled to develop emotional or intellectual connections, and what might that tell you about the variability of your target audience?

Plus-One Approach: A Quick Review

We explored this approach back in chapter 4. Here's a quick reminder of the steps:
- Choose the learning experience.
- Identify the biggest pinch point.
- Hypothesize the barrier.
- Design a countermeasure.
- Try it out.
- Reflect on results.

You can apply this to a presentation, an onboarding workshop, an instructional video—any learning experience in which you have a clear goal and are finding that some learners are struggling to meet that goal. The more you engage in this process, the easier and quicker it becomes. Remember, slow is smooth, and smooth is fast.

You can use the UDL Guidelines to support your empathy and guide your intentional approach.

- **Start with the foundations**. Without learner attention and accessible media, tools, and spaces, the learning is not getting off the ground. So, start by supporting interest, perception, and physical action, and then work to develop your capacity, and that of your learners, to address barriers in the higher elements.

- **Remember, the Guidelines are a lens, not a checklist**. You don't have to develop countermeasures to problems you don't have, so, though you should consider each checkpoint, you don't need to create an option or support for each, only those for which you anticipate presenting a barrier.

- **Check out the appendices**. I've included breakdowns of each Guideline and checkpoint, including loads of examples and strategies. Just remember that this is a framework, not a prescriptive list. You should always consider your context when choosing how best to address barriers to learning.

Paint a New Picture of What Learning "Looks Like"

This shifting of your own practice, changing your perspective on how best to support your learners, is going to cause a shift in the learners. Over time, you'll be changing people's conception of what organizational learning looks like. However, you must be prepared for the variability in your audience to embrace this new paradigm. Remember our novice-expert learner continuum from chapter 2. Some may act like novices because they've not been allowed or supported to do more, while others may be limited by their own mental models of what learning is. We in L&D can and should expect and support them to become expert learners, but we can't expect that transformation to come quickly or easily for everyone.

A really valuable lesson I've learned, though I sometimes need reminding, is that my learners may have different perspectives on their level of ownership. I have found that unless I give explicit permission for them to exercise autonomy, many will revert to the novice learner mode because of prior experiences in training or education. It can be something as simple as seating during in-person learning. In my workshops and presentations, I tell people, "The only thing holding you in your chair is gravity and your choice to stay seated. If you need to get up and stretch, do it. If you need to walk a bit in the back of the room, have at it. As long as what you do doesn't interfere with your ability to learn or the learning of others, I'm good with it." Whether it's seating, choice of partner, method of expression, you name it, look for opportunities to offer choice and build autonomy.

Here's a cautionary tale about what happens when you push learners too far too fast toward expert learning. Several years ago, I was recruited by a professional association to give a three-hour workshop to a group of their members, all mid-level managers from a variety of organizations, as part of an extended series of workshops. In the initial briefing, the director of professional learning, we'll call her Anne, told me that she wanted me to make the experience really engaging and interactive. "These people work all week. The last thing they want on a Friday night is for you to just stand there and do a slide presentation." She also wanted them to cover a lot of content, so she recommended I help them divide and conquer the learning objectives.

With my client's expectations clear, I designed a learning experience that would support autonomy, collaboration, and creative expression. That evening, we examined the learning objectives and constructed a list of learning behaviors we'd need to employ in order to get them all accomplished (e.g., avoiding email, working collaboratively, and so on). They divided themselves into teams, each focusing on a particular area of the night's content. Delving into a variety of learning assets, including videos, articles, and infographics, they constructed and delivered presentations to each other. Some used digital presentation tools such as PowerPoint and Prezi, while others made handouts and used flip charts. Each held a Q&A, and then we came together to give each other constructive feedback and build consensus on the key learning for the evening. Finally, we assessed whether or not we met the learning objectives. Afterward, Anne told me how much she loved the new approach, and she thought the people were really engaged. Unfortunately, we both misread the audience. In reading the feedback forms (aka smile sheets), I was horrified by how scathing some of the comments were.

"This guy wasn't prepared—he made us do all the work."

"I don't work all week to have to work on Friday night. Why couldn't he just do a presentation like everyone else does?"

"I don't need someone telling me I can't check my email; I have a site to run."

Now, not all the reviews were like that; some really enjoyed the way the workshop was designed and felt they learned a lot. However, it was clear I didn't account for the variability in the audience, and my complete departure from their expected norm created a barrier for them, challenging their perceptions of what learning is supposed to look like on Friday nights. I learned a valuable lesson: I have to meet people where they are with their learning, not just where they are as learners. Then I build from there.

One strategy I have found helpful since that night is that, when I anticipate that a design element (co-constructing goals, having them draft plans for effective learning) may conflict with their ideas of what learning is and their role in it, I explain the *why* behind each move, the value of doing things a different way. For example, I often prompt learners to think about how they need to behave—what they need to do, or not do—to get the most out of our time together and to set and share goals for the experience. I say things like, "We're setting goals for our own self-regulation because doing so makes us more mindful of our own behavior and provides some insurance against wasting our own time. Also, research has shown that when we put a goal into the world by speaking it, writing it, or sharing it, we are more likely to achieve it."

By allowing the learners to see inside the design of the learning environment, you can build emotional, intellectual, and strategic connections to how they're learning, not just what they're learning. They are making this happen. They are in control. They can learn how to learn, be mindful of their learning, and use their expert learning skills to learn anything they want.

Track and Reflect on Your Progress

I've said repeatedly that this is a journey. So, how do you know whether you're making progress? There's no standardized assessment I can offer you to measure your proficiency with pinpoint accuracy, but I can offer you some insight on how to gauge your growth in supporting expert learning.

- **Track Your Actions and Observations**. Document what you're doing and what the results are, including the times things don't go as planned. Don't leave it to memory; keep a record you can reference: a Google Doc, a notebook, whatever works for you. Use it as a reference tool for future designs so when you're thinking about potential barriers and countermeasures, you can refer to your notes for inspiration.

- **Engage your learners**. Ask them how the changes you've been making have affected their experiences learning at work. What's working, and why? What could be improved, and do they have ideas for how? This will both inform your effort as well as communicate and reinforce your role as their partner in continuous learning.

- **Go and See**. Watch your learners in action. A performance improvement initiative should always translate into changes in behavior, and it's likely you or someone else close to the work is evaluating the transfer of knowledge and skills. But is that person also looking for expert learning behaviors? Go looking for effective collaboration, peer feedback, convergent-divergent thinking, and so on. If you explicitly train an expert learning skill in your initiative, include that in the evaluation component.

- **Pause and Reflect**. It's great to put your head down and lean into the challenge, but it's also wise to step back, raise your gaze, and look at what you've been able to accomplish and the impact on your learners. What changes do you notice in yourself and the way you think and act in this work? What about your people? Use this reflection to inform your expectations for yourself. Remember, you need to be an expert learner just as much as anyone else, and that means self-regulation.

Find Community in this Work

Gathering, analyzing, and preserving these data are vital, not only to drive your own improvement, but to help you convince others that you're on the right journey and that they should join you. Let's face it: It's hard to be the only person moving in a new direction. There have been many times in my career when I was the first one on my team to begin a fundamental shift in my practice. Whenever possible, I went looking for like-minded folks, internally and externally, so that I could collaborate, exchange ideas and challenges, and draw strength from knowing I was not alone in my belief in finding better ways to help others be their best selves at work.

Now, you may not be ready to enter into, or start, a community to support expert learning. That's okay. Slow is smooth, and smooth is fast. When you reach the point that you want one or more learning partners, come back to this section. Until then, feel free to keep reading or skip ahead to the final note.

External Learning Partners

Let's start with the easy part: engaging in the greater UDL community. UDL has long had a widespread appeal among educators, but now there's a growing number of like-minded folks who are applying UDL to their work in order to build and support cultures of expert learning in organizations. So how do you find them? Here are two quick ways to introduce yourself to other passionate practitioners:

- Join our LinkedIn group Upskill, Reskill, Thrive! - A Group for Fostering Expert Learning", at https://www.linkedin.com/groups/14042404/.

- Follow #UDL on Twitter. You'll certainly find many passionate educators, but also a growing number of learning and development professionals sharing their ideas, examples, and wonderings.

Internal Learning Partners

Now, if you're reading this book as part of a professional learning initiative in your organization, or if it was recommended by a colleague or manager, then you probably have a good idea of whom to talk to as you go forth to do your good work. However, if you're unaware of anyone else who is already engaging in this work, you'll need to do some looking around and maybe some recruiting. With some personal experience and some measurable improvements in outcomes for individuals and teams, you can begin to recruit others to be your learning partners.

This journey is never fully over, so you can start to share your work with others as soon as you're ready. However, many people may not be swayed if all you have to say about this work is "I just finished this book and the author said . . . " Before you go recruiting, I recommend you reflect on your own learning and gauge your readiness to begin leading others down the path.

How will you know whether you are ready? I would recommend two criteria:

- **You've have been deliberately practicing**: You've made several iterations on designs to address barriers to learning and have some measurable improvements that you can at least correlate to your installation of countermeasures.

- **You can explain it simply and clearly**: You feel well versed enough in UDL and expert learning that you can explain the concepts simply and plainly. If you're not sure, try the Feynman technique I shared in chapter 5.

With those criteria met, you can begin building your cohort of fellow UDL practitioners. But whom do you recruit? First, I recommend looking at your fellow L&D practitioners. You can start to build community around the work of facilitating the capacity of others, share ideas and lessons learned, and collaboratively engage in the application of your UDL lens. However, you may not want to start with all your colleagues; more likely you'll need a select few to begin the work. Determining which ones can be tricky and may be counterintuitive.

When working with folks seeking to build expert learning cultures, I met many who wanted to start with the "hardest nuts to crack," that is, the people they thought would resist change the most. The reasoning is understandable: If you can sway the most resistant, everyone else should be easy. Don't do that.

Instead, take inspiration from the work of the late sociologist Everett Rogers, a pioneer in the diffusion of innovations, or how some ideas spread and scale. Chances are you've seen Simon Sinek's 2009 TED Talk "How Great Leaders Inspire Action." (As I write this, that video has 57 million views and counting.[2]) If so, you may remember Simon drawing a Bell curve on poster paper and explaining how to create momentum around an idea or innovation. Whether you're familiar with the video of Rogers' work or not, the answer is simple: Start with the people you likely don't have to convince, the people who are consistently ready to try new things, the people who champion efforts of improvement or inclusion. As Sinek puts it, "People don't buy what you do, they buy why you do it." So, start by appealing to people whose beliefs align with expert learning and innovation.

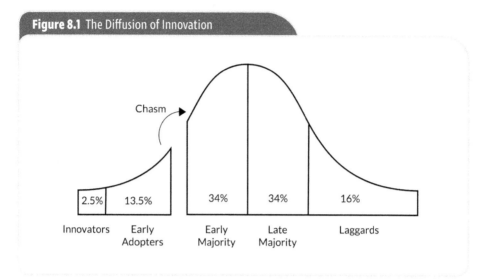

Figure 8.1 The Diffusion of Innovation

Chasm

| 2.5% | 13.5% | 34% | 34% | 16% |

Innovators · Early Adopters · Early Majority · Late Majority · Laggards

I've written this book for those who believe that we can best help our people and organizations by letting our people own their learning and lead us to new ideas and opportunities. Though Universal Design for Learning is based on a myriad of research-based constructs of learning and motivation, I can't give you a case study about how it's transformed a Fortune 500 company. That's how innovation works: You can't be innovative by asking for examples of 10 other times it's been done successfully. I'm counting on the innovators, the people who want to try new things to reinvent how we learn at work, to move this work forward. If you're one of those innovators, you're going to need to find other like-minded folks, people you don't have to convince. You want the people who will need only to be convinced to take it slowly because they're so excited by the idea that they want to do it all immediately.

But how do you know for sure who will be on board and who will resist? You don't. So, consider how you might offer the opportunity to learn about UDL and expert learning to all without requiring it of any. You might:

- Host a series of lunch-and-learns or open-door sessions.

- Share some resources that people can explore if they choose.

- Post ideas and questions on internal comms channels such as Slack or Yammer.

See who takes the bait, and then engage them. Take their questions and offer to share your experiences if they're interested.

> ## Starting a Movement at Walmart
>
> Kendra Grant is a proponent of expert learning, an author of a book on expert learning, and an L&D practitioner in the field. When she took charge of an L&D unit, she took a measured approach to bringing her new team on board to a new way of thinking.
>
> "I had to go slow," she says, "because when I got there, it was very much – watch this [video], do this e-learning, take this assessment. It was very lockstep."
>
> Kendra began with improving accessibility and by building her team's empathy using learner personas. She also had her team create learning videos, review them to see who would learn from them and who would encounter barriers, and then think up other options.
>
> Building on that, she kept engaging her team in conversations about who their learners are. Most of her team were well read and did well in school, so they might be tempted to design learning for people like them, but that becomes a barrier to diversity.

With your new community, you can begin practicing slowly and deliberately. You can learn from each other's successes and misfires, providing a supportive environment for experimentation. Over time, you can build in examples of your work in action and evidence of impact. These you can use to start convincing those who need a little more assurance about the new ideas you're sharing. Remember, the hallmark of creativity is the process of developing an idea that has value.[3] You'll need some evidence of that value to expand your movement beyond the people who already take the idea on faith.

As for the hardest nuts to crack, the ones who say things like, "I taught the stuff. If they didn't learn it, it's on them" or "transfer is a management problem," you may be able to recruit them with sufficient practice, usually when most everyone else is already on board with the new direction. However, I did mention that one criterion is that you're prepared for disagreement because you should consider that some people will disagree. Do all you can to identify the barriers to their acceptance of new practice. What is getting in their way of change? Are they afraid to fail, or are their mental models so strong that they can't shift them to a new paradigm? In the face of that resistance, don't lower your expectations for their improvement or the ownership of potential barriers to their behavior change. Don't ever stop offering opportunities for them to learn and change. Don't write anyone off. You may find that some barriers beyond your control will erode over time or that those not excited about the cultural change will seek out departments or organizations that cling to a more traditional approach.

Engage Your Leadership

"Leadership" is a term that is used widely and in different ways, so, let's operationally define it for our purposes. In one sense, leadership is the collection of people in positions of high power and influence—the president and the various chief officers, directors, and so on. These are the people in charge, those with the ability to make strategic decisions, create or eliminate systems and processes, and so forth. These are the people we need on our side if we are really going to change the culture of the organization because when people want to know what the organization really stands for, they look at what these people say and do.

I want to focus on a different definition of leadership, one focused on influence rather than hierarchical position. World-renowned author and researcher Brené Brown defines a leader as "anyone who takes responsibility for finding the potential in people and processes, and who has the courage to develop that potential."[4] When we actively seek to improve and innovate, and to recruit and support others to that end, we are being leaders, no matter our title. We can lead laterally, engaging our colleagues. We can lead down the chain, supporting and guiding individuals and teams we've been selected to manage. But we can also lead up the chain, supporting the decisions of key personnel and recruiting their support for organizational change and improvement.

To create and sustain a culture of expert learning, you will have to assume a leadership role in that work. As before, there's no one right way to do this, but I will share some ideas based on my experiences and the input of those I interviewed for this book.

Before we begin, let's address why we need the traditional leadership, high-ranking people in the organization, on our side. We need them to give us the grace and space to try new things, to devote resources to the work, and to communicate their support of the effort. But more than that, we need them to model the culture we seek and to intentionally address barriers to its creation. Put simply, we need them to believe in this work, tell people they believe it, and then act like they believe it.

So, how do we get leadership on our side? Just as we learned in the last section, people are more likely to support change that furthers the causes they already champion. If we are to recruit leadership to this cause, it's helpful to examine what they already believe about learning and then draw connections between those beliefs and the cause of expert learning. In chapter 1, I told you about the learning philosophy of the United States Marine Corps, recorded in their doctrinal publication MCDP 7 – Learning. Every marine, no matter how high or low in the organization, is expected to continuously learn and improve and to support other marines to do the same. This is made clear to everyone both inside and outside of the organization.

What's your organization's learning philosophy? What does your leadership believe about the need for continuous learning and improvement of individuals and teams? How do you know? Here are some good places to start looking:

- **Learning Philosophy/Statement**: Is there a document or some portion of the vision and mission statement that explicitly supports continuous improvement?

- **Leadership Reports and Presentations**: What have the CEO, president, and other senior leaders stated about learning at work? Look for annual reports, state of the organization addresses, and other high-profile communications for emphasis on learning and innovation. Whom do they invite to speak at retreats or to the general staff, and what are those messages?

- **Leadership Learning Material**: What are they reading, listening to, or watching to drive their own improvement, and what lessons are contained in those materials? From whom are they drawing their inspiration and information, and what might that tell you about what they believe? For example, if your executives are exploring the work of Amy Edmondson, you might infer that they are appreciative of the need for psychological safety.

- **Daily Communications**: What are leaders sharing in their day-to-day communications that might hint at their willingness to embrace the work of expert learning? What are they saying in emails, on Yammer or Slack, or on their LinkedIn profiles? In many cases, you can look at someone's social media and get a good sense of what they believe just by surveying what they say, or don't say.

Looking at some or all of the above sources of information, you may be able to identify a couple of members of the leadership group that you won't really have to convince. Once you do that, consider taking the following steps:

1. **Get on Their Radar**. Invite them to lunch, request a meeting, or engage them through social media. Get their attention however you can.

2. **Appeal to Their Purpose**. Build an emotional connection. "Wouldn't it be great," you might say, "if we could create an environment where people could continuously learn and improve so that they win and we win? What if learning was something they owned, and we supported, instead of something we did to them or expected to happen by accident?"

3. **Share and Connect the Big Ideas**. Now for the intellectual connection. Illustrate, as simply and clearly as you can, the concept of expert learning and ask them to think of a time they behaved that way. People who reach high levels in organizations are likely to identify with the need to be purposeful and motivated, knowledgeable and resourceful, and strategic and goal directed. Then, make the connection to the organization. What might it look like to have an organization full of expert learners? How much better equipped would we be to advance our shared vision? Give them some ideas of what this "looks like" now, and what it might look like down the road. Provide them with information on what you and your budding community have been able to accomplish so far and what the impact has been. However you can, draw a clear line between expert learning and organizational benefits.

4. **Get Strategic**. Engage them in a discussion of what learning currently looks like in their organization. Support your new partner to begin thinking in terms of goals, barriers, and countermeasures, and examine the current culture in those terms. If the goal is a culture of expert learning, how do current behaviors, practices, and systems align, or misalign, with that goal? How might we begin to make changes? Come prepared with examples,

but be ready to collaboratively diagnose barriers to hypothesize initial countermeasures.

5. **Establish Clear Expectations**. Focus on going slow to eventually go fast. Identify areas to pilot countermeasures. Rather than going big to start, go for some easy wins, areas that require low effort but yield measurable impact. This will reinforce the value of the work and build expectations of success for future endeavors, both key elements of engagement that we explored earlier in chapter 5.

Final Note

You are what's needed to improve the performance of individuals and teams in your organization. You understand the innate variability of learners, the impact of context on learning, and that barriers exist in the learning environment, not the learner. You can leverage the UDL Guidelines to engage the affective, recognition, and strategic networks, the holy trinity of learning, to foster and sustain learning.

You are ready to partner with your learners, to support their ability to be expert learners. You can create environments that are born accessible, inspire ownership, support collaboration and creativity, and lead to authentic transfer to boost individual, team, and organizational performance. You can show all your new partners that learning is something L&D does *with them*, not *to them* or *for them*.

Fostering expert learning takes a short time to begin and a lifetime to master, but you've put in the work to begin your deliberate practice. Don't worry about doing it all, just do something, see what happens, and then adjust. Please consider joining our growing community on LinkedIn. We want to hear about your first steps, your successes, and your lessons learned. Bring us your ideas and your questions; we can engage in expert learning together.

Reflect and Connect

- Look back on your learning to this point. Have your perceptions of learning, and your role in supporting learning, shifted over the course of this book? What aha moments stick out, and what questions remain?

- You're moving forward on your UDL journey, so, consider your next step. Where might you begin to Plus One your current work? Who might want to join you in your new learning?

Resources

- "Why Great Employees Leave 'Great Cultures'" by Melissa Daimler. Short version: No amount of foosball or free salad can overcome the belief that your organization doesn't walk its talk. So, if you want to examine the role leaders play in defining and aligning culture, this article provides a workable framework. You can find it at https://hbr.org/2018/05/why-great-employees-leave-great-cultures. *Harvard Business Review* allows access to three articles/month for free; after that, you'll need a subscription.

- *How Great Leaders Inspire Action.* Simon Sinek's TED Talk remains an accessible and applicable approach to communicating ideas and recruiting support for your cause. This video includes a great primer on Emmet Rogers' Diffusion of Innovations theory. You can add to the more than 57 million views by going to https://www.ted.com/talks/simon_sinek_how_great_leaders_inspire_action.

Resources

1. "TR Center - TR Quotes - Do What You Can with What You've Got Where You Are." *Theodore Roosevelt Center,* https://www.theodorerooseveltcenter.org/Learn-About-TR/TR-Quotes/Do%20what%20you%20can%20%20with%20what%20you%20ve%20got%20%20where%20you%20are?from=https%3A%2F%2Fwww.theodorerooseveltcenter.org%2FSearch%3Fr%3D1%26searchTerms%3Ddo%2520what%2520you%2520can. Accessed 22 Mar. 2021.

2. Sinek, Simon. *Start with Why: How Great Leaders Inspire Everyone to Take Action.* 2013.

3. Robinson, Ken, and Lou Aronica. *Creative Schools.* Penguin, 2016.

4. Brown, Brené. "Dare to Lead Hub." *Brené Brown,* 2022, https://brenebrown.com/hubs/dare-to-lead/.

USING THE UDL GUIDELINES IN THE WORKPLACE

The purpose of this appendix is to explain the *what* and *how* of applying the Universal Design for Learning Guidelines to the workplace. As I mentioned briefly in chapter 3, the UDL Guidelines were originally formulated for formal learning environments and have been applied primarily to educational settings such as Pre-K–12 and, more recently, to higher education. However, as you've discovered, the Guidelines help us establish, maintain, and enhance that learning triangle that is vital for any meaningful change, including in the workplace. If you've read the rest of this book, you know *why* to use these Guidelines, and you understand the conceptual frameworks that serve as the basis for them. You also may have some ideas, based on some of the examples, your own experiences, and your reflections on the concepts, as to what UDL might look like for you on Day 1. The UDL Guidelines can help you on Day 1 and every day after as you progress on your journey.

The UDL Guidelines

The UDL Guidelines, seen in figure A.1, are vertically and horizontally arranged and have varying levels of complexity.[1] Add in some unfamiliar terminology and they can be somewhat bewildering at first take. Therefore, let's break them down and make them navigable so you can use this appendix effectively. Go to udlguidelines.cast.org for various printable versions.

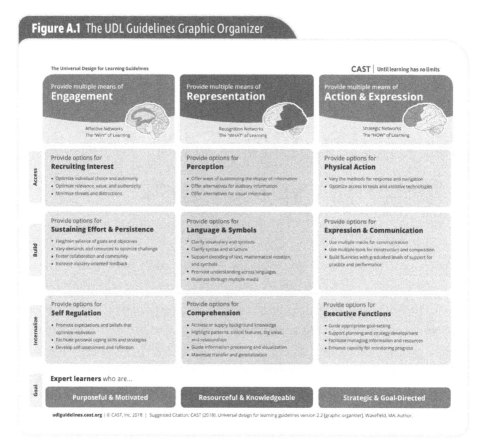

Figure A.1 The UDL Guidelines Graphic Organizer

The Universal Design for Learning Guidelines

CAST | Until learning has no limits

Provide multiple means of
Engagement

Affective Networks
The "WHY" of Learning

Provide multiple means of
Representation

Recognition Networks
The "WHAT" of Learning

Provide multiple means of
Action & Expression

Strategic Networks
The "HOW" of Learning

Access

Provide options for
Recruiting Interest
- Optimize individual choice and autonomy
- Optimize relevance, value, and authenticity
- Minimize threats and distractions

Provide options for
Perception
- Offer ways of customizing the display of information
- Offer alternatives for auditory information
- Offer alternatives for visual information

Provide options for
Physical Action
- Vary the methods for response and navigation
- Optimize access to tools and assistive technologies

Build

Provide options for
Sustaining Effort & Persistence
- Heighten salience of goals and objectives
- Vary demands and resources to optimize challenge
- Foster collaboration and community
- Increase mastery-oriented feedback

Provide options for
Language & Symbols
- Clarify vocabulary and symbols
- Clarify syntax and structure
- Support decoding of text, mathematical notation, and symbols
- Promote understanding across languages
- Illustrate through multiple media

Provide options for
Expression & Communication
- Use multiple media for communication
- Use multiple tools for construction and composition
- Build fluencies with graduated levels of support for practice and performance

Internalize

Provide options for
Self Regulation
- Promote expectations and beliefs that optimize motivation
- Facilitate personal coping skills and strategies
- Develop self-assessment and reflection

Provide options for
Comprehension
- Activate or supply background knowledge
- Highlight patterns, critical features, big ideas, and relationships
- Guide information processing and visualization
- Maximize transfer and generalization

Provide options for
Executive Functions
- Guide appropriate goal-setting
- Support planning and strategy development
- Facilitate managing information and resources
- Enhance capacity for monitoring progress

Goal

Expert learners who are...

| Purposeful & Motivated | Resourceful & Knowledgeable | Strategic & Goal-Directed |

udlguidelines.cast.org | © CAST, Inc. 2018 | Suggested Citation: CAST (2018). Universal design for learning guidelines version 2.2 [graphic organizer]. Wakefield, MA: Author.

How to Read the Guidelines

The highest level of organization is the **principle**, each corresponding to a network. The **Principles of Engagement, Representation, and Action and Expression** address the affective, recognition, and strategic networks, respectively. They are arranged in columns left-to-right, however, no hierarchy is intended. Just like the networks they support, each principle is applicable throughout any learning event.

Figure A.2 The Three UDL Principles

Provide multiple means of
Engagement
Affective Networks
The "WHY" of Learning

Provide multiple means of
Representation
Recognition Networks
The "WHAT" of Learning

Provide multiple means of
Action & Expression
Strategic Networks
The "HOW" of Learning

Each principle is divided into three **Guidelines** in bold print, providing more specific guidance within the overall principle. Beneath each Guideline is a bulleted list of **checkpoints**, representing more detailed suggestions. For example, the Guideline **Recruiting Interest** has three checkpoints: "Optimize individual choice and autonomy; Optimize relevance, value, and authenticity; and Minimize threats and distractions."

The Guidelines are also organized in horizontal rows, beginning with the **Access** row. Access is the baseline for our work, suggesting ways to foster initial interest, perception, and physical accessibility.

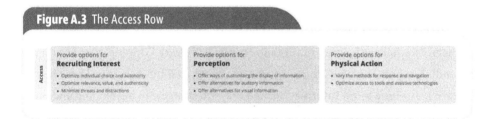

Figure A.3 The Access Row

Access

Provide options for
Recruiting Interest
• Optimize individual choice and autonomy
• Optimize relevance, value, and authenticity
• Minimize threats and distractions

Provide options for
Perception
• Offer ways of customizing the display of information
• Offer alternatives for auditory information
• Offer alternatives for visual information

Provide options for
Physical Action
• Vary the methods for response and navigation
• Optimize access to tools and assistive technologies

The **Build** row does just that, leveraging the initial work of the access row and further driving engagement, representation, and action and expression.

Figure A.4 The Build Row

The **Internalize** row focuses on empowering people to own their learning through self-regulation, making connections to work and prior learning, and executive functions.

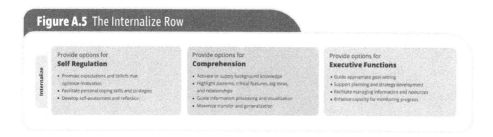

Figure A.5 The Internalize Row

The **Goal** row declares the intent of UDL: To produce and support expert learners. As you have learned in this book (or will, if you're skipping ahead to this appendix), **expert learners** are purposeful and motivated to learn, they know how to learn and where to get information, and they are strategic in developing and using their learning to achieve their goals. These are the types of learners we need in organizations. These folks can persist in the face of challenges, transfer learning into practical application, and communicate their learning to others.

Figure A.6 Goals of Expert Learners

Though the Guidelines progress vertically downward, this should not imply that the Access row Guidelines and checkpoints are necessarily easier than those further down. For example, let's consider the checkpoint Minimize Threats and Distractions. That's talking about the ability to focus, which is always important. Minimizing threats relates to the need for psychological safety, which is a whole field of study and the subject of many articles and books. So, higher up doesn't mean easier.

The rows also should not be interpreted as "do the top, then the middle, then the bottom." They are all in play, all the time. Think about that same checkpoint: Threats and distractions are never good and should be addressed throughout the learning process, not just in the initial recruitment of interest.

How to Use the UDL Guidelines

There is a misconception among new practitioners that the Guidelines *are* UDL. UDL is a way of thinking and operating, having clear, challenging goals, anticipating barriers in learners' pursuit of those goals, and providing flexibility through options and supports so that learners can meet or exceed the goals. The Guidelines are a tool that can help us do that by directing our attention to likely areas where barriers might be present and giving us a general directive through Guidelines and checkpoints.

As you may have noticed, the Guidelines and checkpoints are phrased as actions—support, guide, facilitate, minimize, and so on. They tell us that if we anticipate a barrier, we must **do** something because we own the environment, barriers and all. However, they don't tell us precisely how; that would be too prescriptive. We get to decide how to do that, based on our capacity, our strengths, and our context.

I use these Guidelines all the time. I frame discussions with them, and I work with teams and organizations to make them part of their common language. It's how we talk about learning, and the more familiar they become, the more quickly and effectively we implement them in our learning and working environments. What follows is a row-by-row expansion on each Guideline and checkpoint to help inform what UDL might look like for you when dealing with a barrier. It is not meant as a prescriptive list or an encyclopedia of every potential countermeasure.

The Access Row
Engagement: Provide Options for Recruiting Interest

We now know that we can't learn anything without first paying attention, and to gain and sustain attention, we need people to feel like the learning is worth doing and that they can be successful. The first Guideline in the **Principle of Engagement**, "Provide Options for Recruiting Interest," seeks to address barriers to the learner's initial search for why to promote an initial eagerness to learn.

Checkpoint	Big Idea for L&D	UDL might look like
Optimize individual choice and autonomy.	Having a choice allows people to play to their strengths and interests, increasing their expectation of success. It communicates that people are being respected enough as adults to make those choices for themselves.	• Laying out problems without suggesting solutions, leaving the challenge open to all ideas. • Offering options for building knowledge and skills (e.g., in-person workshop, online training, job shadow, book study). • Offering options for demonstrating learning (e.g., writing, oral review, demonstration).
Optimize relevance, value, and authenticity.	People engage in learning that they perceive is worth doing. People will vary in their perceptions of the value of a task, and some may need support in finding and embracing the why of the learning.	• Allowing participants to bring an authentic, relevant problem of practice into the learning event as a focus for applying the learning. • Having participants generate what improved performance might look like in their context and what is needed to get there. • Sharing examples of authentic application. • Highlighting performance improvements after learning events and again before new events to demonstrate the real-life positive impact of learning.

Minimize threats and distractions.	Threats make us avoid learning and stick to what we think are safe behaviors. Distractions divert our attention away from the learning. We need to identify and mitigate potential threats and distractions in the learning environment.	• Removing unnecessary presentation elements (flashy visuals, unrelated audio, and so on) that can potentially distract the learner from the task at hand.

• Modeling focused attention by putting your phone away or turning away from your screen to converse.

• Acknowledging the existence of outside pressures and identifying appropriate times and methods for learners to "check in" with life outside the learning.

• Allowing for varied publicity of performance. For example, allow for private assessment instead of in front of a crowd of peers or managers.

• Modeling respect for diverse opinions and privacy so that all voices can be heard without fear of reprisal from you or others.

• Giving explicit permission to try new things and sharing examples of learning from failure. |

Representation: Provide Options for Perception

We can't learn information we can't access, and we know there is variability in the ways individuals take in information. This first Guideline in the **Principle of Representation** focuses on supporting that variability so learners have a chance to access information so they can then process and retain it.

Checkpoint	Big Idea for L&D	UDL might look like
Offer ways of customizing the display of information.	People vary in the pace at which they can take in information. Further, we may need information enhanced or streamlined so we can better access it. Providing options and tools can help eliminate barriers to perception.	• Providing materials in advance of meetings, workshops, and presentations so that people can review information at their own pace. • Providing materials electronically so they can be accessed with enhanced accessibility tools such as magnification and contrast controls. • Recording meetings and webinars and providing other notetaking supports so people can focus on processing rather than archiving information.
Offer alternatives to auditory information.	Auditory information, especially in more than short bursts, is very hard to remember verbatim. Further, variability in hearing, either because of innate challenges or conflicting noise in the environment, can make auditory information inaccessible.	• Using symbols, gestures, and other visual cues to mirror or emphasize verbal information. • Providing printed instructions for all workshop activities, work processes, and daily assignments. • Ensuring all images and videos have detailed captions. • Following up meetings, coaching sessions, performance reviews, and project reviews with an email or note summarizing feedback and next steps. • Providing written transcripts for videos and audio clips.

| **Offer alternatives to visual information.** | People rely heavily on sight for processing their surroundings. However, visual information is not always the most accessible information, particularly when there are language barriers or other abstractions involved, let alone a physical impairment.

A spoken word may be more decipherable than a written one, both for a language learner as well as someone with dyslexia or some other visual processing challenge. Therefore, it's best to offer auditory representations whenever possible. | • Providing audio or Braille versions of manuals, memoranda, and job aids.

• Providing descriptions (text or spoken) for all images, graphics, video, or animations.

• Providing access to text-to-speech (TTS) programs to convert written text to auditory information. |

Action and Expression: Provide Options for Physical Action

This first Guideline in the **Principle of Action and Expression** establishes the baseline of access with an aspiration to continuously address barriers in pursuit of that blue-sky aspiration, learning environments that are truly born accessible. For the workplace, we would want to expand our scope to examine not only the methods and tools but also the physical spaces where work, and learning, happen.

Checkpoint	Big Idea for L&D	UDL might look like
Vary the methods and pace for response and navigation.	We don't all think, let alone communicate, at the same speed. Further, biases can lead to prioritizing some voices and ideas over others. We want to intentionally address barriers so that everyone has the opportunity and ability to engage meaningfully in communication and ideation. Learners employing accessibility supports may require more time to communicate and navigate both digital and physical environments, so we need to anticipate that variability if we are to be effective learning partners.	• **Providing wait time**. Make sure you give everyone a chance to process by challenging them to think for about 5 seconds before responding. • **Allowing the option to report back**. If a person or group finds themselves at a loss for an answer, give them the option to report back when they have gotten further in their learning rather than offering the opportunity up to others. • **Removing unnecessary time constraints**. Unless there is a specific reason for speed, remove speed from the equation. This will reduce both stress and errors. • **Looking for missing voices**. Monitor meetings and communications to determine whether there are people and views that are not being heard. • **Ensuring compliance with state and federal accessibility requirements**.

Optimize access to tools and assistive technologies.	We must ensure that there are no physical barriers preventing people from engaging meaningfully in learning and work. If some of our people can't physically manipulate a tool or navigate an environment, they can't do their best work unless we provide them access to viable options and supports.	• **Including novices and experts in the design process** to get informed perspectives on learning environment accessibility. • **Providing guidance** for using accessibility tools. • **Journey mapping user experiences** to detect and address barriers. • **Selecting software that works seamlessly** with keyboard alternatives and alt keys.

The Build Row
Engagement: Sustaining Effort and Persistence

Expectations of success and perceptions of value are always important, not just at the beginning. This second Guideline in the **Principle of Engagement** capitalizes on that initial recruitment of interest by continuing to reinforce the value of the learning and keep those expectations of success alive.

Checkpoint	Big Idea for L&D	UDL might look like
Heighten the salience of goals and objectives.	People will vary in their ability to maintain their connection to the value of the learning. We must continuously support their connection to a meaningful why so that they feel as though their efforts are worthwhile.	• **Offering frequent opportunities to stop and review goals and objectives** ("Let's remember why we're working so hard. . . .") • **Drawing a clear line** between the immediate work and the ultimate goal. • **Recognizing individual and team contributions** in pursuit of the goals. • **Sharing authentic user stories** that demonstrate the potential positive impact of the work ("Because of the work you do here, James can now . . .")

Vary demands and resources to optimize challenge.	Our learners are variable in their experiences, skills, and mindsets. We want to closely monitor and adjust the level of challenge so that we boost, rather than dampen, engagement.	• **Allowing repeated attempts** to demonstrate proficiency. • **Prompting/modeling the use of available supports** so it's clear to all that there are resources available to them. • **Pairing novices with those with more expertise**, which can positively affect the engagement, and learning, of both.
Foster collaboration and community.	Just as lifting a heavy object is easier with more helping hands, collaboration can make challenging learning easier on everyone involved by distributing the mental weight and harnessing the group's processing capacity. Further, strong teams can reinforce individual belonging and expectations for success, fueling greater engagement in learning and work.	• **Referring to ideas and challenges as "ours"** instead of "yours" or "mine." • **Modeling ownership** of the overall challenge rather than "I did my part." • **Highlighting collective accomplishments** after they happen and when introducing new challenges. • **Reviewing pending work collaboratively** where team members assign themselves work and volunteer to collaborate with others to get things done (e.g., a daily standup meeting). • **Emphasizing the importance of sharing knowledge**. • **Creating time and space** for sharing to happen.

| Increase mastery-oriented feedback. | Effective feedback informs actions and expectations of success. When we know what's working, what's not working, and the why of both, we can take meaningful action to continue what's working and fix what's not. | • **Providing frequent, objective reviews** of performance.

• **Building opportunities for peer feedback** during team meetings and project reviews.

• **Asking questions that prompt self-assessment** (e.g., "Why did you do it that way?").

• **Reviewing team progress collaboratively**.

• **Soliciting feedback** from others.

• **Modeling** both delivery and acceptance of feedback.

• **Providing examples and non-examples** of effective feedback. |

Representation: Provide Options for Language and Symbols

This second Guideline in the **Principle of Representation** supports our learners' ability to make sense of the information being presented efficiently and effectively. We can support this by providing clarity and connection and by chunking the learning into digestible pieces.

Checkpoint	Big Idea for L&D	UDL might look like
Clarify vocabulary and symbols.	Jargon, esoteric terminology, and domain-specific symbols can all impede understanding; further, they can alienate people. Overly complex instructions create barriers to comprehension and execution.	• **Using simple language** and avoiding acronyms, abbreviations, and jargon whenever possible. • **Embedding support for unfamiliar references** (e.g., domain-specific terms or notations, idioms, jargon). • **Using an active voice.** • **Including the goal** in the instructions.

Clarify syntax and structure.	Structures that use language or symbols in specific orders or relationships need to be clarified. For instance, if we are coding priorities by color (red = emergency), we need to explicitly communicate the meaning and implications of each color.	• **Providing keys, legends, or other resources** to support interpretation of specific structures and systems. • **Pairing system-specific language with plain speak.**
Support decoding of text, mathematical notation, and symbols.	Learners will vary in the pace at which they can process complex groupings of terms based on prior knowledge, vision, and more.	• **Ensuring digital content is accessible and navigable** (e.g., alt-text for pictures, structured headings). • **Providing text-to-speech supports.**
Promote understanding across languages.	When people have to translate information into their native language, that's an increased demand on their ability to process that information. Therefore, we need to support that translation effort, or remove its necessity, in order to best support processing.	• **Making key information in the dominant language** (e.g., English) **also available in the first languages** (e.g., Spanish) **for learners with limited proficiency** in the dominant language and in ASL for learners who have difficulty hearing. • **Linking key terms to definitions and pronunciations** in the dominant and heritage languages. • **Providing electronic translation tools** and access to multilingual glossaries. • **Avoiding idiomatic expressions.** • **Embedding visual, nonlinguistic supports** for clarity (pictures, videos, and so on).

| Illustrate through Multiple Media. | Relying solely on written or spoken language can present barriers to understanding. Showing people what you're talking about can eliminate these barriers. | • **Pairing text**, especially lengthy or complex passages, with visuals (pictures, diagrams, storyboards) that clearly illustrate the same message.

• **Providing opportunities for hands-on or 3-D learning** (mock-ups, examples, miniatures, virtual/ augmented reality). |

Action and Expression: Provide Options for Expression and Communication

The second Guideline in the **Principle of Action and Expression** helps us engage the strategic networks of the brain, fostering the application of new knowledge through ideation, experimentation, demonstration, and discourse.

Checkpoint	Big Idea for L&D	UDL might look like
Use multiple media for communication.	Not everything is an email or a slide presentation. Unless the point is to demonstrate mastery of a single method of communication (e.g., writing), encourage people to communicate in multiple ways, allowing them to play to their strengths as well as assess what might best communicate their message.	• **Using discussion boards, social media, and other digital tools** to provide asynchronous or anonymous communication of ideas, questions, and feedback. • **Providing multiple communication pathways** for input and feedback. • **Modeling a variety of communication methods** to establish the viability and validity of each.

Use multiple tools for construction and composition.	If the product is a written document, does it matter if we create that through typing, speech to text, or digitized handwriting? Rather than limiting expression to a traditional tool or method (e.g., typing), provide alternative methods of engaging in a method of expression, thereby eliminating potential barriers and opening up possibilities for all.	• **Providing a variety of physical or digital tools** for communication and creating evidence of learning, including speech-to-text and audio video recording. • **Providing exemplars and other scaffolds** to aid in construction.
Build fluencies with graduated levels of support for practice and performance.	People's familiarity with different tools and methods of communicating is variable. For instance, technology changes all the time, so some may not be up to date on the latest collaborative tools and design programs. It's not enough to give people access to new tools; you need to make sure there are supports available to help those who need them.	• **Providing access to tutorials and tip sheets** to help people build familiarity with new tools. • **Encouraging experienced peers to support novices** to learn the new processes and skills. • **Giving real-time, actionable feedback** to help learners refine their skills. • **Providing exemplars of effective communication** with annotations describing what makes them good examples.

As stated in chapter 7, you may want to enhance your efforts by expanding your gaze to include supporting the generation of ideas along with the expression and communication of those ideas. Experience, perception, and other factors bring us variability in people's capacity to be creative—to have original ideas that have value—individually and as a team. As such, I recommend you build learner capacity and provide the context necessary so that your people can create choices (divergent thinking) and then make choices (convergent thinking). This might include:

- **Allowing for private brainstorming** followed by a group review of ideas. This prevents one or two voices from dominating the ideation based on their comfort with sharing and the speed of their generation.

- **Providing a gap between convergent and divergent thinking**. Allow a set time for ideation. Then, introduce a break. When learners return to their list of ideas, they'll be more ready to start whittling down to viable options.

- **Endorsing and modeling experimentation** and the learning that comes from both success and failure.

- **Setting norms for collaborative convergent thinking**. Make sure all praises and criticisms are directed at ideas, not people. Promote shared ownership of selected ideas.

- **Allowing time and space for innovation to happen**. They can't fail intelligently if you don't let them, so don't swoop in with solutions. Ask leading questions and challenge your learners to come up with solutions.

The Internalize Row
Engagement: Provide Options for Self-Regulation

UDL takes the concept of the self-regulation cycle and converts it into practical applications so that we can incorporate them in our designs and our working environments. We're continuing to enhance expectations of success, develop ownership of performance improvement, build capacity to self-monitor, and adjust behaviors to optimize performance and deal with challenges to improvement.

Checkpoint	Big Idea for L&D	UDL might look like
Promote expectations and beliefs that optimize motivation.	Learners needs to believe that they can and should learn. We want to identify and address barriers to those beliefs so that every learner expects to improve and knows that learning comes from what they do rather than what is done to them.	• **Encouraging people to be learn-it-alls** rather than know-it-alls.[2] • **Sharing examples of authentic growth** and improvement as models (e.g., "They did it, and you can, too."). • **Celebrating mini-successes** and the contributions of individuals and teams that produced those results. • **Helping learners to identify areas of strength** that can be leveraged for individual and team achievement.
Facilitate personal coping skills and strategies.	Real growth takes effort and grit. We can anticipate that there will be challenges with staying on task, persisting through challenges, self-reflection, and so on, so be proactive in supporting people to push through when the learning gets tough.	• **Modeling self-awareness** and calling attention to your use of coping mechanisms. • **Normalizing challenge** so that people feel safe in seeking help. • **Encouraging decompression strategies** like mindfulness breaks, stretching, and breathing exercises. • **Establishing and reinforcing norms** for civil discourse. • **Creating safe channels** for communicating negative emotions and dissenting opinions.

| Develop self-assessment and reflection. | We want to support learners' metacognition — thinking about their thinking — so they can reliably assess their current knowledge and skill as well as their role in achieving, maintaining, and elevating that level of proficiency. | • Routinely **asking reflective questions**.

• **Providing reference points** (data, exemplars, and so forth) so learners can accurately gauge their own performance compared with the desired outcome.

• **Connecting people to learning resources and programs** available through the organization.

• **Explicitly communicating that learning is part of work**, not something done outside or instead of work.

• **Providing regular opportunities for self-assessment and goal creation/ revision**. |

Representation: Provide Options for Comprehension

This final Guideline in the **Principle of Representation** targets barriers to long-term memory integration and retention, allowing us to support our variable learners to process new information, connect it with their existing understanding, and apply that learning to solve authentic problems.

Checkpoint	Big Idea for L&D	UDL might look like
Highlight patterns, critical features, big ideas, and relationships.	As we learned in chapter 6, novices and experts vary in the pace at which they can process new information. Helping learners, particularly novices, see the big picture and the interconnections between key pieces allows them to home in on critical information rather than be overwhelmed with minutiae. This makes learning more efficient by reducing the friction caused by disorganized information.	• **Using bold or color-coded text and headings** to draw the eye to key information and demonstrate relationships. • **Providing summary points**. • **Using examples as well as non-examples** to drive the key points home. • **Use visuals and tools** (diagrams, concept maps, graphic organizers, flow charts) to demonstrate key concepts and relationships. • **Providing opportunities** for learners **to identify or generate connections**.

Guide information processing and visualization.

When faced with complex content, it helps to break the information down so as not to overwhelm anyone. Start simple and then progress toward the complex. Break your content into chunks so learners can progress at a manageable rate. Helping learners orient themselves to where they connect to the content can also support better processing. Provide visuals (thinking maps or concept diagrams) that represent connections between big ideas.

- **Separating complex processes or systems into distinct components**, covering each part's specific vocabulary and function and then exploring how these elements interact.

- **Priming learners for processing** by explicitly tying new information to previously covered material.

- **Avoiding seductive details that distract** people from the learning (e.g., flashy graphics or outlandish analogies).

- **Providing visual or physical models** so people can better understand processes and systems by observing their operation.

- **Presenting information in tables, charts, or infographics.**

| **Maximize transfer and generalization.** | Our learners must connect what they learn from us to their performance on the job, so we need to identify and eliminate barriers to that transfer. There should be no mystery as to the applicability of the learning, and we shouldn't assume people will naturally make the necessary connections to effectively use the learning on the job. | <ul><li>**Drawing clear connections between content and workplace performance**.</li><li>**Providing materials and resources that can be readily used in the flow of work**, thus, providing support when and where it's needed.</li><li>**Offering or soliciting examples and non-examples** of authentic, effective application.</li><li>**Engaging in scenario-based exercises** such as simulations or hypothetical questions. Scenarios are particularly effective because they provide<ul><li>a safe environment for initial practice of new skills;</li><li>a realistic context for the application of new skills; and</li><li>the opportunity for immediate feedback.</li></ul></li></ul> |

Action and Expression: Provide Options for Executive Functions

This Guideline works hand-in-hand with the other two Guidelines in this row. As you'll see, we're looking at the strategic effort to further knowledge and skills, in other words, how we attempt to actualize. These efforts are fueled by engagement, but they are also informed by knowledge. Thinking strategically requires you to project what could happen if you acted, and those predictions rely on your understanding of the factors at play.

Checkpoint	Big Idea for L&D	UDL might look like
Guide appropriate goal setting.	Continuous improvement comes from setting goals and working to meet or exceed them. Whether in a formal learning setting or on the job, we can support learners to set goals for applying their learning, allowing for variability in capacity and context.	• **Starting with a pre-assessment of the target knowledge and skills** and letting your learners score their own work using a key or rubric. • **Providing reference points for proficiency (or even excellence)** through exemplars or rubrics so people know what success looks like. • **Having frequent, informal progress reviews** so you collaboratively assess current performance, next steps, and overall progress toward the goal. • **Communicating expectations** for learning and transfer. • **Providing frameworks for setting effective goals**, such as SMART (strategic, measurable, attainable, relevant, time-bound) or FAST (frequent, ambitious, specific, transparent).

Support planning and strategy development.	People may encounter barriers in determining how to cross the chasm between where they are and where they want to be. We can support them to orient themselves to the task at hand and think and act strategically to complete it.	• **Providing process guides that detail the pathways to success**. Chart the known paths to success. • **Building time in the schedule for progress monitoring** so people can assess their status, make necessary adjustments, and select next steps. • **Highlighting common pitfalls** so people can avoid "learning the hard way" without constraining them to one path. • **Providing planning tools and templates** so they can map out their plans and keep track of actions taken and next steps.
Facilitate managing information and resources.	People need to know where to find the knowledge, tools, and other assets necessary to develop, carry out, and revise their plans.	• **Providing toolkits and templates** that can provide curated resources and guidelines without overloading learners. • **Providing overviews of supports** so learners know what they have at their disposal as well as how, where, and why the supports are helpful. • **Building capacity to navigate knowledge banks** by helping learners understand where and how to access necessary information.

Enhance capacity for monitoring progress.

Information is key to execution, both in supporting self-control and mental flexibility (executive functions) as well as reinforcing our emotional commitment to the endeavor (self-regulation). Supporting learners to access information that is timely, coherent, and actionable allows them to gauge and adjust their effort and actions.

- **Providing progress indicators** such as agendas, progress bars, and other signals to highlight progress through the learning event.

- **Providing guidelines and templates** for learners to take and use for self-assessment.

- **Offering options** for feedback types and channels.

- **Highlight progress** through use of pre- and post- assessments, graphs, and charts showing progress over time.

Bibliography

Almarode, John. "Success Criteria: An Essential (and Often Underutilized) Component of Teacher Clarity." *Corwin Connect*, 3 Feb. 2021, https://corwin-connect.com/2021/02/success-criteria-an-essential-and-often-underutilized-component-of-teacher-clarity/.

"Americans with Disabilities Act of 2008." *U.S.C.*, 110–325, 25 Sept. 2008.

ATD Research. *2020 State of the Industry: Talent Development Benchmarks and Trends*. Association for Talent Development (ATD), 2020, p. 60.

Atkinson, R., and R. Shiffrin. "Human Memory: A Proposed System and Its Control Processes." *The Psychology of Learning and Motivation: Advances in Research and Theory*, vol. 2, Academic Press, 1968.

Authors@Wharton Speaker Series Presents Satya Nadella. Directed by Wharton School, 2018. *YouTube*, https://www.youtube.com/watch?v=gnFzQDjU5YQ.

Bartlett, Michelle, and Ehrlich, Suzanne. How a Universal Design Mindset can support learning in the workplace. *Ahead,* November, 2019

Battarbee, Katja, et al. *Empathy on the Edge: Scaling and Sustaining a Human-Centered Approach in the Evolving Practice of Design*. IDEO, 2014, https://new-ideo-com.s3.amazonaws.com/assets/files/pdfs/news/Empathy_on_the_Edge.pdf.

Beich, Elaine. *The Art and Science of Training*. ATD Press, 2017.

Bersin by Deloitte. *Leading in Learning: Building Capabilities to Deliver on Your Business Strategy*. Deloitte, https://www2.deloitte.com/content/dam/Deloitte/global/Documents/HumanCapital/gx-cons-hc-learning-solutions-placemat.pdf.

Bersin, Josh. "A New Paradigm For Corporate Training: Learning In The Flow of Work." *JOSH BERSIN*, 3 June 2018, https://joshbersin.com/2018/06/a-new-paradigm-for-corporate-training-learning-in-the-flow-of-work/.

Bersin, Josh, and Marc Zao-Sanders. "Making Learning a Part of Everyday Work." *Harvard Business Review*, 19 Feb. 2019. *hbr.org*, https://hbr.org/2019/02/making-learning-a-part-of-everyday-work.

Brown, Brené. "Dare to Lead Hub." *Brené Brown*, 2022, https://brenebrown.com/hubs/dare-to-lead/.

Butler, Paul. *Training and Leading at Newleaf*. 2 Sept. 2021.

Cable, Dan. *Alive at Work: The Neuroscience of Helping Your People Love What They Do*. Harvard Business Review Press, 2019

CAST. *UDL & the Learning Brain*. CAST, 2018, http://www.cast.org/products-services/resources/2018/udl-learning-brain-neuroscience.

---. *Universal Design for Learning Guidelines Version 2.2*. 2018, https://udlGuidelines.cast.org/.

CEUD. "What Is Universal Design." *Centre for Excellence in Universal Design*, http://universaldesign.ie/What-is-Universal-Design/. Accessed 30 Mar. 2020.

Chang, Jie. "A Case Study of the 'Pygmalion Effect': Teacher Expectations and Student Achievement." *International Education Studies*, vol. 4, no. 1, Jan. 2011, p. p198. *DOI.org (Crossref)*, https://doi.org/10.5539/ies.v4n1p198.

Cleese, John. *Creativity: A Short, Cheerful Guide*. Crown, 2020.

Chick, Nancy. "Metacognition." *Vanderbilt University*, 2013, https://cft.vanderbilt.edu/guides-sub-pages/metacognition/.

CNBC.com, Susan Caminiti, special to. "AT&T's $1 Billion Gambit: Retraining Nearly Half Its Workforce for Jobs of the Future." *CNBC*, 13 Mar. 2018, https://www.cnbc.com/2018/03/13/atts-1-billion-gambit-retraining-nearly-half-its-workforce.html.

Cockerell, Lee. *Creating Magic: 10 Common Sense Leadership Strategies from a Life at Disney*. Vermilion, 2009.

Daimler, Melissa. Why Great Employees Leave "Great Cultures". *Harvard Business Review*, May, 2018

Defelice, Robyn. *How Long to Develop One Hour of Training? Updated for 2017*. 9 Jan. 2018, https://www.td.org/insights/how-long-does-it-take-to-develop-one-hour-of-training-2017.

Defeyter, Margaret Anne, et al. "The Picture Superiority Effect in Recognition Memory: A Developmental Study Using the Response Signal Procedure." *Cognitive Development*, vol. 24, no. 3, July 2009, pp. 265–73. *ScienceDirect*, https://doi.org/10.1016/j.cogdev.2009.05.002.

"Definition of Executive Function | Dictionary.Com." *Www.Dictionary.Com*, https://www.dictionary.com/browse/executive-function. Accessed 31 May 2021.

Doerr, John. *Measure What Matters: How Google, Bono, and the Gates Foundation Rock the World with OKRs*. Protfolio/Penguin, 2018.

Dresler, Martin, et al. "Mnemonic Training Reshapes Brain Networks to Support Superior Memory." *Neuron*, vol. 93, no. 5, Mar. 2017, pp. 1227-1235.e6. *ScienceDirect*, https://doi.org/10.1016/j.neuron.2017.02.003.

Dweck, Carol S. *Mindset*. 2017.

"Ecosystem." *Encyclopedia Britannica*, https://www.britannica.com/science/ecosystem. Accessed 29 Sept. 2020.

Edmondson, Amy. "Psychological Safety and Learning Behavior in Work Teams." *Administrative Science Quarterly*, vol. 44, no. 2, June 1999, p. 350. *DOI.org (Crossref)*, https://doi.org/10.2307/2666999.

Edmondson, Amy C., and Per Hugander. "4 Steps to Boost Psychological Safety at Your Workplace." *Harvard Business Review*, 22 June 2021. *hbr.org*, https://hbr.org/2021/06/4-steps-to-boost-psychological-safety-at-your-workplace.

Egan, D. E., and B. J. Schwartz. "Chunking in Recall of Symbolic Drawings." *Memory and Cognition*, vol. 7, 1979, pp. 149–58.

Ekman, Rolf, et al. "A Flourishing Brain in the 21st Century: A Scoping Review of the Impact of Developing Good Habits for Mind, Brain, Well-Being, and Learning." *Mind, Brain, and Education*, vol. 16, no. 1, Feb. 2022, pp. 13–23. *ERIC*, https://doi.org/10.1111/mbe.12305.

El-Boustani, Sami, et al. "Locally Coordinated Synaptic Plasticity of Visual Cortex Neurons in Vivo." *Science*, vol. 360, no. 6395, June 2018, pp. 1349–54. *DOI.org (Crossref)*, https://doi.org/10.1126/science.aao0862.

"Empathy." *Merriam-Webster Online*, https://www.merriam-webster.com/dictionary/empathy.

Ertmer, Peggy A., and Timothy J. Newby. "The Expert Learner: Strategic, Self-Regulated, and Reflective." *Instructional Science*, vol. 24, no. 1, Jan. 1996, pp. 1–24, https://doi.org/10.1007/BF00156001.

Federal Aviation Administration. *Air Traffic By The Numbers*. 27 May 2022, https://www.faa.gov/air_traffic/by_the_numbers/.

Fiske, S., and S. Taylor. *Social Cognition*. McGraw-Hill, 1991.

Fuchs, Eberhard, and Gabriele Flügge. "Adult Neuroplasticity: More Than 40 Years of Research." *Neural Plasticity*, vol. 2014, 2014, p. 541870. *PubMed Central*, https://doi.org/10.1155/2014/541870.

Funahashi, Shintaro, and Jorge Mario Andreau. "Prefrontal Cortex and Neural Mechanisms of Executive Function." *Journal of Physiology-Paris*, vol. 107, no. 6, Dec. 2013, pp. 471–82. *ScienceDirect*, https://doi.org/10.1016/j.jphysparis.2013.05.001.

"Genchi Genbutsu." *Lean Enterprise Institute*, https://www.lean.org/lexicon-terms/genchi-genbutsu/. Accessed 6 June 2022.

Glossary of ADA Terms | ADA National Network. https://adata.org/glossary-terms. Accessed 9 Dec. 2021.

Gobet, F., and G. Clarkson. "Chunks in Expert Memory: Evidence for the Magical Number Four… or Is It Two? Memory." *Memory*, vol. 12, no. 6, 2004, pp. 732–47, https://doi.org/DOI 10.1080/09658210344000530.

Greene, Ross. *Lost at School: Why Our Kids with Behavioral Challenges Are Falling through the Cracks and How We Can Help Them.* 2nd ed., Scribner, 2014.

Groot, Adriaan David Cornets de. *Thought and Choice in Chess.* Mouton, 1965.

Haidt, Jonathan. *The Happiness Hypothesis: Ten Ways to Find Happiness and Meaning in Life.* 2006.

Harvard Business Review. *The Impact of Employee Engagement on Performance - SPONSOR CONTENT FROM ACHIEVERS.* Harvard Business Review, 2013. *hbr. org*, https://hbr.org/sponsored/2016/04/the-impact-of-employee-engagement-on-performance.

Heath, Chip, and Dan Heath. Switch: How to Change Things When Change Is Hard. London: Random House, 2011. Print.

"History Timeline: Post-It Notes." *Post-It®*, https://www.post-it.com/3M/en_US/post-it/contact-us/about-us/. US. Accessed 3 Oct. 2020.

Hudson, William. What is Human-Centered Design? - YouTube video - William Hudson. March 2, 2020. https://www.youtube.com/watch?v=KkUor_NTuDA

IDEO. "Design Kit." *Design Kit: Empathy*, https://www.designkit.org/mindsets/4. Accessed 5 Nov. 2021.

---. *What Is Design Thinking?* https://www.ideou.com/blogs/inspiration/what-is-design-thinking. Accessed 1 Aug. 2020.

"IDEO Design Thinking." *IDEO | Design Thinking. designthinking.ideo.com*, https://designthinking.ideo.com/. Accessed 4 Aug. 2020.

Inamori, Takao, and Farhad Analoui. "Beyond Pygmalion Effect: The Role of Managerial Perception." *Journal of Management Development*, vol. 29, no. 4, Apr. 2010, pp. 306–21. *DOI.org (Crossref)*, https://doi.org/10.1108/02621711011039132.

Initiative (WAI), W3C Web Accessibility. "Keyboard Compatibility." *Web Accessibility Initiative (WAI)*, 3 June 2022, https://www.w3.org/WAI/perspective-videos/keyboard/.

Jain-Link, Pooja, and Julia Taylor Kennedy. "Why People Hide Their Disabilities at Work." *Harvard Business Review*, 3 June 2019. *hbr.org*, https://hbr.org/2019/06/why-people-hide-their-disabilities-at-work.

Kadakia, Crystal, and Owens, Lisa M.D. *Designing for Modern Learning: Beyond ADDIE and SAM*. ATD Press, 2020

Kelley, Tom, and Littman, Jonathan. *The Ten Faces Of Innovation: Ideo's Strategies For Beating The Devil's Advocate & Driving Creativity Throughout Your Organization*. Doubleday, 2005.

Kierein, Nicole M., and Michael A. Gold. "Pygmalion in Work Organizations: A Meta-Analysis." *Journal of Organizational Behavior*, vol. 21, no. 8, 2000, pp. 913–28. *Wiley Online Library*, https://doi.org/10.1002/1099-1379(200012)21:8<913::AID-JOB62>3.0.CO;2-#.

Kirschner, Paul A, and Carl Hendrick. *How Learning Happens: Seminal Works in Educational Psychology and What They Mean in Practice*. Routledge, 2020.

Kruse, Kevin. "What Is Employee Engagement." *Forbes.Com*, 22 June 2012, https://www.forbes.com/sites/kevinkruse/2012/06/22/employee-engagement-what-and-why/#6507480d7f37.

Land, George, and Beth Jarman. *Breakpoint and beyond mastering the future today*. HarperBusiness, 1992.

Learning – APA Dictionary of Psychology. https://dictionary.apa.org/learning. Accessed 26 Nov. 2021.

"Learning Curve." *Lexico Dictionaries | English. www.lexico.com*, https://www.lexico.com/definition/learning_curve. Accessed 1 Aug. 2020.

Livingston, J. Sterling. Pygmalion in Management. Harvard Business Review, January, 2003

Lipp, Doug. *Disney U: How the Disney University Develops the World's Most Engaged, Loyal, and Customer-Centric Employees*. McGraw-hill Education, 2013. Lisa Owens; Crystal Kadakia. *Designing For Modern Learning*. Association For Talent De, 2020.

Marine Corps Doctrinal Publication 7: Learning. MCDP 7, United States Marine Corps, p. 87, https://grc-usmcu.libguides.com/research-topics/main/usmc-doctrine. Accessed 19 June 2020.

Marquardt, Michael J. *Building the Learning Organization: Mastering the 5 Elements for Corporate Learning*. Davies-Black, 2002.

Mayer, Richard E. *Applying the Science of Learning*. Pearson/Allyn & Bacon, 2011.

Meyer, Anne, et al. *Universal Design for Learning: Theory and Practice*. 1st ed.,

CAST Professional Publishing, 2014.

Miller, Earl K., and Timothy J. Buschman. "Working Memory Capacity: Limits on the Bandwidth of Cognition." *Daedalus*, vol. 144, no. 1, Jan. 2015, pp. 112–22. *DOI.org (Crossref)*, https://doi.org/10.1162/DAED_a_00320.

Miller, George. "The Magical Number Seven, plus or Minus Two: Some Limits on Our Capacity for Processing Information." *The Psychological Review*, vol. 63, no. 2, 1956, pp. 81–97.

Niles, Robert. "Disney Legends Recall Walt Disney and the 'Yes, If....' Way of Management." *Theme Park Insider*, 2009, https://www.themeparkinsider.com/flume/200911/1551/.

Orenstein, David. "MIT Scientists Discovery Fundamental Rule of Plasticity." *MIT News*, 22 June 2018, https://news.mit.edu/2018/mit-scientists-discover-fundamental-rule-of-brain-plasticity-0622.

Panopto. "3 Ways Inefficient Knowledge Sharing Hurts Productivity At Work." *Panopto Video Platform*, 16 Oct. 2019, https://www.panopto.com/blog/how-much-time-is-lost-to-knowledge-sharing-inefficiencies-at-work/.

Phielix, Chris, et al. "Awareness of Group Performance in a CSCL-Environment: Effects of Peer Feedback and Reflection." *Computers in Human Behavior*, vol. 26, no. 2, Mar. 2010, pp. 151–61. *DOI.org (Crossref)*, https://doi.org/10.1016/j.chb.2009.10.011.

Pink, Daniel. *Drive: The Surprising Truth About What Motivates Us*. Riverhead Books, 2009

Pontefract, Dan. *Flat Army: Creating a Connected and Engaged Organization.* 2016.

Quoidbach, Jordi, et al. "The End of History Illusion." *Science*, vol. 339, no. 6115, Jan. 2013, pp. 96–98, https://doi.org/DOI: 10.1126/science.1229294.

Raitner, Marcus. "On Top of Mount Stupid." *Medium*, 7 Oct. 2020, https://marcusraitner.medium.com/on-top-of-mount-stupid-9d38d1569225.

Robinson, Ken, and Lou Aronica. *Creative Schools*. Penguin, 2016.

Schraw, Gregory, and Matthew McCrudden. "Information Processing Theory." *Education.Com*, 2009, https://project542.weebly.com/uploads/1/7/1/0/17108470/information_processing_theory__education.com.pdf.

Schunk, Dale H., et al. *Motivation in Education: Theory, Research, and Applications*. Pearson, 2014.

Sim Sitkin. "Learning through Failure - the Strategy of Small Losses." *Research in Organizational Behavior*, vol. 14, Jan. 1992, pp. 231–66.

Sinek, Simon. *Start with Why: How Great Leaders Inspire Everyone to Take Action.* 2013.

State of the American Workplace. 1st Edition, Gallup Press, 2017.

State of the Global Workplace. 1st edition, Gallup Press, 2017.

"The Five Keys to a Successful Google Team." *Rework.Withgoogle.Com*, 2015, https://rework.withgoogle.com/blog/five-keys-to-a-successful-google-team/.

Timeline of 3M History | 3M United States. https://www.3m.com/3M/en_US/company-us/about-3m/history/timeline/. US. Accessed 3 Oct. 2020.

Tobin, Thomas, and K. T. Behling. *Reach Everyone, Teach Everyone: Universal Design for Learning in Higher Education.* West Virginia University Press, 2018, https://www.muse.jhu.edu/book/62887.

Tovar-Moll, Fernanda, and Roberto Lent. "The Various Forms of Neuroplasticity: Biological Bases of Learning and Teaching." *Prospects: Quarterly Review of Comparative Education*, vol. 46, no. 2, June 2016, pp. 199–213. *ERIC*, https://doi.org/10.1007/s11125-017-9388-7.

"TR Center - TR Quotes - Do What You Can with What You ve Got Where You Are." Theodore Roosevelt Center, https://www.theodorerooseveltcenter.org/Learn-About-TR/TR-Quotes/Do%20what%20you%20can%20%20with%20what%20you%20ve%20got%20%20where%20you%20are?from=https%3A%2F%2Fwww.theodorerooseveltcenter.

Upskilling: Building Confidence in an Uncertain World. PwC, 2020, https://www.pwc.com/gx/en/ceo-survey/2020/trends/pwc-talent-trends-2020.pdf.

Vaish, Amrisha, et al. "Not All Emotions Are Created Equal: The Negativity Bias in Social-Emotional Development." Psychological Bulletin, vol. 134, no. 3, 2008, pp. 383–403. DOI.org (Crossref), https://doi.org/10.1037/0033-2909.134.3.383.

Van Der Klift, Emma, and Norman Kunc. "Ability and Opportunity in the Rearview Mirror." Working with Families for Inclusive Education: Navigating Identity, Opportunity and Belonging, vol. 10, Emerald Publishing, Limited, 2017.

Voltaire. A Pocket Philosophical Dictionary. 2020. Open WorldCat, https://dx.doi.org/10.1093/owc/9780199553631.001.0001.

"What Is Accessibility?" AEM Center, https://aem.cast.org/get-started/defining-accessibility. Accessed 9 Dec. 2021.

"What Is Learning Experience Design?" Learning Experience Design, https://lxd. org/fundamentals-of-learning-experience-design/what-is-learning-experience-design/. Accessed 29 Aug. 2020.

Willink, Jocko. All Your Excuses Are Lies - Jocko Willink - Bing Video. 7 Aug. 2017, https://www.bing.com/videos/

Index

A

B

C

countermeasures
    designing, 46, 122
    environment, barriers in, 32–38
    implementing, 47
    knowledge management, 113
    ownership improving, 47–48
COVID-19 pandemic
    challenging work spaces, 82
    impact of, 2, 7
creativity process
    defined, 98–99
    flexibility, 101–103
    opportunities for, 99–100
    safety, 100–101
culture of learning, 26–27
curb-cut effect, 96

D

Defelice, Robyn, 14
Defeyter, Margaret Anne, 93
Deloitte, 23
development and delivery time ratio, 11
development professional. *See* learning and development (L&D)
Dictionary.Com, 118
diffusion of innovations, 127–128
Disney, Walt, 44
Disney U, 43
distractions, minimizing, 59
divergent thinking, 101–103, 151
diversity, impacting learning, 18
Doerr, John, 11, 14
Dresler, Martin, 94
Dunning-Kruger effect, 67
Dweck, Carol S., 44, 52
dyslexia, 106, 143

E

Ebbinghaus, Hermann, 89
Edmondson, Amy, 73
efforts, sustaining, 35, 59–65
Egan, D. E., 93
Eichinger, Bob, 24
Ekman, Rolf, 52

G

H

I

informal learning, 25
information processing model (IPM), 75–77
innovation, 7, 127–128
integration, of memory, 87–90
integration, process of, 85
intellectual connections/networks
    brain networks, 29, 53
    environment, 4
    Principle of Representation
        comprehension, 36, 87–90, 138, 153–156
        language and symbols, 36, 80–87, 137–138, 147–149
        perception, 36, 75–80, 137, 141–143
intelligent failures, 64
interest recruitment, 35, 54–59
internal learning partners, 126–130
intrinsic feedback, 60–61
ISTE. *See* Inclusive Learning Network of the International Society of Technology in Education (ISTE)

J

Jain-Link, Pooja, 23
jargon, 84
Jarman, Beth, 117
journey maps, vi, 30–31, 42

K

Kadakia, Crystal, 118
Katja, Battarbee, 51
Kennedy, Julia Taylor, 23
keyboard functionality, 37
Kierein, Nicole M., 52
Kirschner, Paul A., 92
Kittel, Anne, 67
knowledge management, 113–114
knowledge-sharing, 62
Komawole, Emi, 41
Kruse, Kevin, 73
Kunc, Norman, 100, 117
Kunz, Rebecca, 67

L

memory
    accessibility of, 77–78
    long-term, 77
    long-term memory, 75, 85, 87–90
    sensory memory store, 77
    short-term, 77
    working, 81–82, 109
memory-enhancing mnemonics, 88
mental flexibility, 109, 114
Merriam-Webster Online, 51, 106, 117
metacognitive strategies, 61, 66, 68
Meyer, Anne, 3, 5, 23, 34, 39, 73, 92
Miller, Earl K., 93
Miller, George, 93
mindset
    empathy, 40–43
    expectations (growth mindset), 43–48
    ownership, 28, 48–50
Minnesota Mining and Manufacturing Company (3M), 99, 100–101, 103, 117
model vulnerability, 64
modern learner, traits of, 15–16
modern reality vs. traditional methods, 10–13

N

Nadella, Satya, 7
neurodiversity, 109
Newby, Timothy J., 5
Newleaf Training and Development, 12, 14
Niles, Robert, 52
novice-expert learner continuum, 17, 54, 122
novice learners, 17, 54
Nuclear Power School, 27

O

on-demand learning, 15–16
on-the-job learning, 24–25
Orenstein, David, 52
organizations
    learning philosophy, 13, 14
    needs and goals, 5
Owens, Lisa, 118
Owens-Kadakia Learning Cluster Design model (OK-LCD), 114
ownership, 28, 48–50, 111

P

Q

R

Raitner, Marcus, 74
recognition networks
    brain networks, 20–22
    environment, 32
    Principle of Representation, 34
        Comprehension, 36, 87–90, 138, 153–156
        Language and Symbols, 36, 80–87, 137–138, 147–149
        Perception, 36, 75–80, 137, 141–143
rehearsal, of information, 88–90
relation, of information, 87–88
relevant options, 59
reports, to leadership, 131
representation, principles of. *See* Principle of Representation
reskill, 9
resources, locating and leveraging, 112–113
risk assessment, 54–55
Robinson, Ken, 98, 117, 134
Rogers, Everett, 127
Roosevelt, Theodore, 119
Rose, David, 3, 34, 76

S

safety
    in communication, 107
    creativity process, 100–101
    fostering, vii
    psychological safety, 57–58, 63–64, 111
Schraw, Gregory, 93
Schunk, Dale H., 73
Schwartz, B. J., 93
selection of information, 78
self-control, 109
self-directed learners, 16, 17, 54, 95
self-reflection, 70–71
self-regulated learning (SRL), 67
self-regulation, 35, 65–71, 124, 138, 151–153
sensory memory store, 77
Seufert, Tina, 67
70:20:10 model, 24
Shiffrin, R., 93, 94
short-term memory, 77

traditional methods vs. modern reality, 10–13
transparent goals, 111
trinity, 120–122
turnover, cost of, 9
Twitter, 126

U

UDL. *See* Universal Design for Learning (UDL)
UDL guidelines
  Access row
    perception, 137, 141–143
    physical action, 137, 143–145
    recruiting interest, 137, 140–141
  Build row
    expression and communication, 137–138, 149–150
    language and symbols, 137–138, 147–149
    sustaining effort and persistence, 137–138, 145–147
  checkpoints
    reading, 137
    using, 139
  engaging the three networks, 21–22
  Goals of expert learners row, 138–139
  how to read, 136–139
  how to use, 139–159
  Internalize row
    comprehension, 138, 153–156
    executive functions, 138, 156–159
    self-regulation, 138
  Principle of Action and Expression
    creativity process, 98–104
    executive functions, 37, 108–115, 138, 156–159
    expression and communication, 37, 104–108, 137–138, 149–150
    physical action, 37, 95–98, 137, 143–145
  Principle of Engagement
    recruiting interest, 34, 54–59, 137, 140–141
    self-regulation, 35, 65–71, 138, 151–153
    sustaining effort and persistence, 35, 59–65, 137–138, 145–147
  Principle of Representation
    comprehension, 36, 87–90, 138, 151–153
    language and symbols, 36, 80–87, 137–138, 147–149
    perception, 36, 75–80, 137, 141–143
  See also Universal Design for Learning (UDL)

United States Marine Corps (USMC), 8, 14
Universal Design, 96–97
Universal Design for Learning (UDL)

W

Walmart, v–vi, 129
Walt Disney World, 107
Widener, Billy, 119
WII FM, 56–57
Willink, Jocko, 28, 39, 51
Wilson, Timothy D., 14
working memory, 81, 109
Work Institute, 14
writing, 105–106

Y

Yammer, 113, 128
"yes, if" attitude, 44–45

Z

Zendesk, 113
Zimmerman, Barry, 65–66
Zimmerman, Barry J., 73
Zoom, 7

Acknowledgments

I have so many people to thank for supporting this work, each having made a valuable contribution. Four years ago, Katie Novak encouraged me to pitch the idea to David Gordon at CAST, who has graced me with his support, and his patience, ever since.

Thomas Tobin was an early and enthusiastic thought partner. Numerous business, design, and learning leaders gave me the gift of their time and experience, including (but not limited to): Thomas Amiya, Nairee Bedikian, David Berke, Kristin Brooks, Paul Butler, Fred Cochran, Kasia Derbiszeswka, Valerie Fletcher, Ryron Gracie, Kendra Grant, Maria Grasso, Kavita Gupta, Sam Johnston, Nare Khodadadians, Kevin Kwan, Jennifer Levine, Rebecca Lundeen, Gill McKenna, Scott Millward, Paul Ministrelli, Matt Navo, Valerie Quezada, Sung Park, Josh Safdie, Billy Schleifer, Sujie Shin, Scott Smith, Zach Smith, Keegan Tangeman, Donna Van Allen, and Patrick Veenhoff.

Finally, I would like to express my deep and sincere thanks to my editor and thought partner, Billie Fitzpatrick. We did it!

About the Authors

James McKenna, EdD

James McKenna loves to learn and help others learn and improve. He supports organizations to develop, sustain, and leverage inclusive learning and working ecosystems so that individuals and teams can learn, innovate, and thrive. He is a leader, instructional designer, trainer, and facilitator.

James serves as the assistant director of Professional Learning and Leadership Development at the California Collaborative for Educational Excellence and is the founder of McKenna Learning, a learning and development consultancy. He is a regular speaker at national conferences and leads the development of digital resources to support inclusive learning at scale. Previously, James was a consultant, administrator, and special education teacher for the Los Angeles County Office of Education, a musician, a nightclub doorman, and veteran of the United States Navy. In short, he's worn a lot of hats.

He received a BA in music from the University of Massachusetts – Boston, an MA in education from the University of Phoenix, and an EdD in education leadership with a focus on education psychology from the University of Southern California. He is also certified as a master instructional designer by the Association for Talent Development (ATD).

A native of Revere, Massachusetts, James currently lives in the Los Angeles area with his wife, Janine, and his children, Juliet and Jack.

Kendra Grant

Kendra Grant's first career (and love) was in K–12 education. She was a teacher, teacher-librarian, district special education coordinator, and assistive technology specialist in a large school district. Her second career, as the cofounder and chief education officer for a professional learning company, focused on UDL and technology implementation.

Today, in her third career, Kendra's goal is to bring UDL to the workplace. Through intentional, inclusive design, her goal is to help companies move away from one-size-fits-all corporate training to help every employee develop learner expertise and reach their maximum potential. She was senior manager of learning design and delivery at Walmart, and now is principal of her own L&D practice. Kendra holds a master's of educational technology degree from the University of British Columbia. She is a past president of ISTE's Inclusive Learning Network and was honored to be the recipient of the Outstanding Inclusive Educator award in 2019.

CPSIA information can be obtained
at www.ICGtesting.com
Printed in the USA
BVHW052343280223
659402BV00015B/851